ALL THE WAY TO THE BANK

Smart Money Management for Tomorrow's Nonprofit

THE STEVENS GROUP

Financial Management Consultants

ALL THE WAY TO THE BANK
Smart Money Management for Tomorrow's Nonprofit

Authors: Susan Kenny Stevens and Lisa M. Anderson

Production and design: Brenda A. Christoffer, The Stevens Group
Cover design: MacLean & Tuminelly
Printed by: Edwards Brothers, Inc.

Published by: The Stevens Group, Inc.

First Edition

Printed in the United States of America

ISBN 0-9652208-7-7

This publication is designed to provide accurate and authoritative information in regard to the subject matter covered. It is sold, however with the understanding that it is not intended either to offer or to be a substitute for legal, tax, or investment advice. If such advice or assistance is required, the services of a competent professional should be sought.

TABLE OF CONTENTS

MAKING THE MOST
OF WHAT YOU HAVE

For my thirteenth birthday I received a jewelry box—the multi-tiered kind with separating trays meant to hold an assortment of necklaces, bracelets, and rings. Unfazed by the fact that I had no jewelry, I elevated my new treasure, with its lock and key, to the status of *bank,* and into it I placed all my weekly baby-sitting earnings.

As I progressed through my teenage years and was expected to pay more of my own way, my double-decker jewelry box, with its large lower coffers and its upper divided units, moved from mere locked-box status to a functional cash manager for my earnings and obligations.

Once each week I'd size up my holdings, project my needs for upcoming activities, and allocate the appropriate amount to various top-shelf dividers. Little did I know that with that weekly transfer of funds from one deck of my makeshift bank to another, I had become a money manager.

Twenty years later, I enrolled in an executive development program through Cornell University's Business School—a six-week immersion in finance, accounting, and economics. I had just been promoted to be the administrator of a nonprofit health care agency. In addition to learning the ins and outs of that agency's complicated financial systems, my promotion happened at the same time the HMO movement hit the until-then fairly stable world of health care.

At Cornell, I realized I was not alone in my quest to get a crash course in financial know-how for difficult times. Other mid-level executives were there for the same reason. The difference between them and me (if you don't count budget size!) was that I was the only nonprofit manager in a class of 120 oil, timber, and manufacturing corporate executives.

Nonetheless, what I was learning about money was as valuable to me and my nonprofit agency as it was to them and their Fortune 500 Corporations—maybe more valuable, if you believe in the economics of scarcity.

Within a year, armed with my adapted business school know-how, I launched The Stevens Group, a financial management company committed to strengthening nonprofit organizations through sound, practical, strategic advice about money. And although the Cornell experience was an invaluable boundary-spanner for me personally, in many ways it simply reinforced my earlier instincts as a "jewelry box" money manager: *The less you have, the more you need to make of it.*

And so with the help of Lisa Anderson, my co-author, I've written this book to help nonprofits make the most of the money they have. We'll show you what we've learned from our work with hundreds of nonprofits that have become very smart about money—things like how to take stock of your organization's financial picture, how to strategically manage your cash, the importance of surpluses to financial stability, how and when to borrow money, and how to develop a partnership with your local bank. Along the way we'll introduce you to key financial terms and concepts (refer to the glossary and index for quick reference) and help you discover various strategies to make the most of your financial resources.

What you *won't* find in this book is a chapter on how to raise money—not because it isn't important, but because managing the money you already have is equally important as learning to attract more. If billion-dollar corporations zealously manage their mega-assets, how much more important it is for nonprofits to be smart about their small, but equally precious, funds. *The less you have, the more you need to make of it.*

Although many have contributed to our firm's pool of financial knowledge, I'd be remiss not to acknowledge the more than 500 nonprofits, banks, and foundations across the United States and Canada we've been privileged to advise through the years. We are also indebted to the Otto Bremer Foundation, who commissioned this book. Finally, a special note of thanks is due The Minneapolis Foundation, whose loan programs have given us a special insight into the world of nonprofit money management, and the Bush Foundation, whose 1981 investment in me as a Bush Fellow started it all.

Susan Kenny Stevens
June 1997

SMART MONEY MANAGEMENT
FOR TOMORROW'S NONPROFIT

Mission may be every nonprofit's *raison d'être*, but money is its life blood. Despite the wealth of volunteer labor and goods that so generously pervade the nonprofit sector, it still takes money to deliver both cultural and social programs with the quality and consistency demanded by today's society.

Yet money has always been in short supply for the nonprofit sector. As society's original entrepreneurs, nonprofits have typically faced more demand for their services than they could ever hope to provide. Whether educating children, nursing the elderly, creating cultural programs, or restoring economic vitality to distressed communities, lack of funds has been a major and consistent historical stumbling block.

Understanding Nonprofit Income

Money comes into a nonprofit organization in several different forms. Government and foundation grants, private donations, and other charitable contributions have been the industry's traditional source of funds. Accountants refer to this type of income as *support*. Historically, charitable organizations have relied so heavily on outside support that, for many nonprofits, the word *funding* has become a generic term for income.

Yet, beginning in the early 1980s and continuing into the 1990s, once plentiful public funds sharply decreased. Nonprofit managers joined the entrepreneurial wave that swept the nation and introduced the concept of earned income into their revenue mix.

The ability to generate income from contracts or service fees gave nonprofits a much needed method of diversifying their support base. No longer solely reliant on grant writing and fundraising, nonprofits saw that charging fees for their services could provide a more immediate and controllable source of income.

A revenue-based approach brought with it a different set of financial implications. Words like *billing, collection,* and *accounts receivable* took their place in the nonprofit lexicon right alongside *proposals, case statements,* and *restricted funds.*

Although generating fees gave nonprofits the ability to diversify income, it brought its own share of unpredictability. Now, instead of worrying only about *who* would fund how much of a project, nonprofit managers began to add the question of *when* cash would arrive from services already performed.

As nonprofits entered this world of cash flow, they quickly became a new market for financial services beyond the requisite checking and savings accounts. Nonprofits, just like any growing business, needed cash management services, lines and letters of credit, and a variety of asset management and working capital products to keep them financially solvent and prepared for the future.

Later in this book, an entire chapter is dedicated to services available from your local bank. Too few nonprofits realize the economic benefits that a solid bank partnership can bring them. Instead, many nonprofits have learned only how to develop and foster philanthropic and donor relationships. Every day across the country, classes and seminars are offered on how to attract more funds. All the major nonprofit journals and magazines have grantsmanship as their focus. Everywhere you turn, the nonprofit field is consumed with the philanthropic dollar. Where to get it. How to get it. Who's got it. Who's getting it.

What no one talks about is how to manage it!

Smart nonprofit managers realize that attracting capital to support their missions is going to be harder in the future than it was in the past. They confront this reality by making the most of what they have, paring down expenses where they can, and looking elsewhere for funds needed to break even.

Why Nonprofits Need Banks Now More Than Ever

Some 20 years have passed since the Reagan era brought the first waves of entrepreneurism into the nonprofit marketplace. Although banks and other financial institutions are coming out with more attractive and user-friendly advertising every day, neither the nonprofit nor the financial services industry has yet taken full advantage of the potential benefit each is to the other.

Most individuals in the financial services industry know little about the nonprofit world or how nonprofits conduct their "business." They have no idea that in the United States alone there are more than 1 million nonprofits that employ 15 million people and contribute $500 billion to the annual economy [Source: Independent Sector's *1996-1997 Nonprofit Almanac*].

Instead, some banks still see nonprofits as "small potatoes," voicing uncertainty about the reliability of nonprofit revenues, particularly government contracts and grants. They question nonprofit management practices and fail to understand the nuances of nonprofit fund balances, or *net assets* as they are now called.

Nonprofits, on the other hand, are virtually unaware of how they could use banks and other financial service providers to maximize their resources and make the most of hard-earned cash. Although quick to look under every other stone for new sources of cash, many nonprofits have no idea of the range of financial service options available from their local bank. Worse yet, their own suspicion and mistrust keep them from creating a financial partnership that could be most beneficial if approached from a position of strength.

Since most mistrust stems from what we don't know, let's take a short course on the types of financial institutions that exist in the general marketplace. That way you can match your own money management needs not only to the bank that's most convenient to you, but to one that meets your philosophical and financial specifications.

The Financial Services Industry in a Nutshell

The financial services industry is a multi-billion dollar agglomeration of banks, savings and loans, credit unions, and a host of other less traditional but rapidly expanding service providers: brokerage firms, investment management companies, insurance companies, and community lenders.

In today's convenience-oriented marketplace, you'll find financial services everywhere you go. You can deposit and withdraw money at any time of the day or night, anywhere in the country, in what yesterday would have seemed like the most unlikely places: gas stations, movie theaters, convenience stores. What's more, financial institutions have established retail mini-branches in local grocery and department stores, in airports, and on college campuses to provide services with "real people" rather than the automatic teller type. Individual and institutional investors can buy and sell stocks on the Internet, dial into their local bank for retail services, and pay bills without ever writing a check. What a world!

Although the financial services umbrella grows larger every day, nonprofits have historically relied upon three key institutions for their financial requirements: commercial banks, savings and loan associations, and credit unions.

Commercial Banks—Among the variety of players in the financial services industry, the dominant financial institution remains the commercial bank. There are more than 12,000 banks in the United States alone. All of them share two essential characteristics: they accept demand deposits (checking accounts) and they make commercial loans. Bankers refer to this combination of functions as a "full-service institution." Legally speaking, a financial institution cannot be considered a bank if it does not meet these basic requirements.

As commercial entities, banks have shareholders, who require a certain return on investment. If federally chartered, banks are regulated by the Comptroller of the Currency. Those that are state chartered are controlled and regulated by their state's banking commission. The Federal Deposit Insurance Corporation's (FDIC) Bank Insurance Fund insures deposit accounts in federally insured banks for up to $100,000 per depositor.

Savings and Loan Associations—Savings and loan associations (S&Ls) were originally called "building societies" because their primary and traditional focus was on mortgage lending. Despite the highly publicized crisis of the 1980s and their subsequent multi-billion dollar bailout, S&Ls continue to be the largest source of mortgage credit for individual homeowners. The FDIC's Savings Association Insurance Fund (SAIF) insures deposit accounts in federally insured savings and loans for up to $100,000 per depositor.

Nonprofits searching for bank services in today's financial services economy will find it hard to distinguish between the products of an S&L and those of a commercial bank. Their products are nearly identical. A word to the wise, however: don't use the term "S&L" in the same breath as "bank" when talking to a commercial banker. You and I may not see the distinction, but within the industry, these are still considered two distinct types of institutions.

Credit Unions—Credit unions are nonprofit "cooperatives" that provide financial services to their members. Credit unions exist for social and fraternal groups, civic associations, and branches of the armed services. Most credit unions are comprised of individual members. However, if the members of a membership-based nonprofit belong to a particular credit union, the organization itself may also qualify to use the services of that credit union.

Originally, the primary function of credit unions was to make loans to individual members, using capital from their members' pooled savings. Today, credit unions offer their constituents a much broader range of services.

As a nonprofit corporation, credit unions' "profits" are tax exempt. Rather than paying a dividend to shareholders as other types of financial institutions do, credit unions apply a portion of their profits to offset interest charged to members for loans, or to offer more attractive rates of interest for deposit accounts. The National Credit Union Administration's

(NCUA) Share Insurance Fund insures deposit accounts in federally insured savings and loans for up to $100,000 per depositor.

Any of these financial institutions will have the basic money management services that nonprofits require, and each offers a degree of safety for your deposits. Chapter 3 further explores the services and products typically offered by banks, as well as the pros and cons of big-bank versus small-bank services.

As a nonprofit, you are by no means limited to banks, savings and loans, or credit unions for financial services. Various other financial institutions offer attractive products for nonprofits seeking maximum return on their resources.

Brokerage Accounts—Insurance companies, commercial finance companies, and investment firms offer various money management accounts and financial services to individual and corporate consumers. These institutions typically pay a higher rate of interest to investors, yet may also attach higher "loads," or fees, to the investment. Likewise, deposits in these types of institutions are not insured against loss by any governmental agency. Except for cash management accounts, the price and dividends of these investment products will fluctuate on a fairly consistent basis. What you've invested at $25 a share may pay you only $22 a share when you liquidate. Consequently, many nonprofit boards and managers shy away from brokerage accounts, fearing they will take a loss of principal and possibly violate their fiscal prudence mandate.

As more and more nonprofits develop 403(b) or 401(k) retirement options for their employees, they will enter the world of insurance company and brokerage firm investing. Chapter 5 takes a further look at how to select an investment account.

Community Development Financial Institutions—Over the last decade, various other financial resources have sprung up around the country offering nonprofits an alternative to the commercial financial services previously mentioned. All major cities, and increasingly many smaller communities, are home to community and economic development organizations that provide low-interest loans and gap financing for disadvantaged communities. These alternative loan funds typically offer more favorable rates and terms than commercial institutions. Because they are not federally regulated, they may also take a concessionary, or less-secured, collateral position on their loans.

Don't assume, however, that this type of financing will be easier to get than from a bank. Typically, the loan review process on noncommercial funds involves as much scrutiny as the bank's. Just like a bank, community development lenders require evidence that you can repay their loan.

Foundations and government entities also sponsor loan and economic development funds specifically for nonprofit borrowers unable to access credit from traditional institutions. For instance, in Minnesota, the Minnesota Nonprofits Assistance Fund (MNAF) provides loans to non-bankable nonprofits for cash flow, working capital, equipment, and facilities-related projects. In New York, the Nonprofit Facilities Fund provides loans and advice to nonprofits for leasehold improvements, facility acquisition, new construction, and energy conservation measures.

Variations of these types of funds exist in other urban locales. In regions where nonprofit loan funds don't exist, some foundations, such as the Otto Bremer Foundation, have begun making *program related investments*, or loans at concessionary rates, to nonprofits for projects that have a designated repayment source.

Today's financial institutions—commercial banks, savings and loan associations, credit unions, commercial finance companies, and alternative financial institutions—have many products to help your nonprofit organization maximize its resources and stabilize uneven cash flow. Finding the right "bank" for you will be the subject of a later chapter. For now we're more concerned that you recognize that managing your money is as important as attracting it—and that banks and other financial institutions are a critical part of the management equation for tomorrow's nonprofits.

▼

IF NONPROFITS COUNTED

We've borrowed the title for this chapter, double meaning and all, from economist Marilyn Waring's book *If Women Counted*. The double entendre sums up the complex financial reality of today's nonprofit economy—an economy that, historically, has placed more value on the sector's *worthiness* than on its *worth*. Some of this may stem from the nonprofit name itself. Nonprofits exist to fulfill their missions, not to earn a profit for their executives, directors, or members.

Nonprofit organizations come in all shapes and sizes. They include local churches and synagogues, large hospitals, human service agencies, professional associations, arts organizations, sports leagues, museums, colleges, and foundations. Some nonprofits operate on shoe-string budgets with no full-time paid staff. Others look remarkably like large corporations with multi-million dollar budgets and sophisticated operating systems.

What makes nonprofits different from their for-profit brethren? In a private or publicly held corporation, owners and shareholders benefit from the firm's profits. Nonprofits, however, must use any surplus of income over expenses—otherwise known as *profit*—to further fulfill the organization's mission. In a nonprofit, no one owns the right to share in the organization's profits or surpluses; it all goes back to the organization for mission-related work.

In the United States, tax laws define nonprofits as groups organized for charitable or mutual-benefit purposes. More than 1 million organizations, representing the majority of nonprofits in the country, have achieved tax-exempt status under the Internal Revenue Code. In addition to being exempt from income taxes, many nonprofits are also exempt from sales and real estate taxes, depending on local regulations. Gifts to many, although not all, nonprofits are also tax deductible for donors, providing an added benefit for both the organization and its contributors.

In 1994, the nonprofit sector accounted for approximately 8 percent of the gross national product, pumping $500 billion into the national economy [Source: Independent Sector's *1996-1997 Nonprofit Almanac*]. In the same period, the sector employed 15 million people—11 percent of the total United States labor force—with wages and salaries topping $200 billion. By any standard, the economic contribution of the non-profit sector is both substantial and impressive. Yet the pervading senti-ment still exists that, at least from a financial standpoint, nonprofits "don't count."

To count means to have value. Webster defines value as "to be strong or worthy." Most nonprofits have the "worthy" part down pat. They've spent a professional lifetime demonstrating worthiness to individual donors and philanthropic and government funders. What some haven't learned is how to think about, talk about, or demonstrate their value to society—in other words, their *worth*.

Yesterday's Reality

To fully understand the complexity of nonprofit worth, we must debunk five long-held tenets associated with the nonprofit world.

Mission is More Important Than Market. Let's be clear. Mission *is* important. Every year, successful nonprofits spend hours revisiting mission statements that articulate why they exist, who they're meant to serve, and how they benefit society. But every mission needs a market to provide its reason for being. In that way, *mission*—who you want to be—is actually secondary to *market*—what society needs from you.

For nonprofits, the word *market* has a second meaning. Not only must the community need your service, someone also must pay for it. That "payer" is frequently a party other than the service recipient. Mission can't exist without market, and for most nonprofits that means money.

Nonprofits Can't Make Profits. As tax-exempt entities, nonprofits exist for a "higher good." Their primary purpose is to better society rather than increase the financial worth of their executives, directors, or members.

Does that mean nonprofits can't make a profit? On the contrary. Smart nonprofits know the value of carryover surpluses to their fiscal stability and plan them into their annual budgets. To avoid confusion, they stay away from the term *profit* and think instead about *surplus* or *excess revenues.*

Nonprofits Must Have Balanced Budgets. Another twist on the "can't have profits" theme is the myth that balanced budgets are a must. Clearly, a nonprofit's budget must project sufficient income to cover anticipated expenses. That should be a given. But it does not hold true that non-profit budgets can't project a surplus or contain a contingency factor to cover inevitable changing circumstances. Planning for contingencies is one of the first signs of smart money management.

The budget is an internal tool, a best guess at how much income and expense is necessary to successfully meet your organization's annual operating plans. There's nothing to prevent you from developing a surplus as part of your annual goals and including that in your current year's budget.

Deficits are Better Than Surpluses. Our better judgment tells us this isn't true. Yet nonprofits that must raise money from foundations and the government frequently worry that their annual surpluses will disqualify them as grant recipients.

In philanthropy, need will always be a fundamental selling point. But need and deficits are two very different things. As dollars get tighter and more nonprofits clamor for the philanthropic dollar, contributors will invest in organizations that have a chance to be around awhile, not those who financially run on empty.

Income is More Important Than Assets. Perhaps the biggest myth of all is that attracting capital is more important than managing it. You'll notice that nowhere in this book do we talk about how to attract more income. Instead, we focus on how to manage what you have. We've taken an asset approach, not because income isn't important. Of course it is. But for most nonprofits, income is the one thing over which they have least control. Our goal is to help you manage what is within your control.

There are numerous books and seminars for nonprofits on fundraising, grantsmanship, and donor relations. In fact, any nonprofit literature search would yield a listing of thousands of books, the majority of which are about how to increase income through one fundraising technique or another. All of these books will help you increase your income, but few will increase your bottom line.

Too many nonprofits fall into the small business trap of defining their financial worth by sales, not by profit. They measure financial success by how much money they raise, rather than the two-pronged goal of how the money they raise benefits the community and, at the same time, improves their own ability to move into tomorrow on solid financial footings.

Tomorrow's reality will belong to those nonprofits who are as interested in increasing their net worth as they are concerned about attracting income.

Getting Real About Financial Worth

There are two primary tools for determining your nonprofit's financial worth: the balance sheet and the income statement. All but the smallest nonprofits prepare these financial documents on a monthly or quarterly basis. Yet these tools are among the most overlooked financial indicators of a nonprofit's performance, stability, and success.

You're probably wondering why we haven't included the budget as a primary tool. The budget—the nonprofit industry's most universally prepared and accepted financial instrument—is certainly an important vehicle for projecting income and expense. But as such, it is useful only as a road map. For nonprofits, the budget's "rubber" meets the proverbial road at the point when actual income and expenses are compared to what was projected. In some cases, that may be at the end of the fiscal year, or at the end of a shorter time frame if plans have changed for the better or worse.

The budgeting process, although universally dreaded, is among the most consistent nonprofit rituals. Yet shifting economic conditions make budget development and review anything but routine.

Most nonprofits approach budget development first from the expense side. Once expenses are formulated, they then tackle income projections. Here things get a little more unpredictable. In the past—with a little help from multiple-year grants, prior years' surpluses, and ongoing revenues—nonprofits could fudge their way into a balanced budget by creating a catch-all "fundraising" line item for the remaining dollars needed to break even. Then, with their budgets neatly balanced and the board's blessing in hand, they'd go forth and spend, confident that one way or another they'd realize the income necessary to support their approved budget's expenses.

Today, funding patterns have changed. Renewable annual donations and reliable percentage increases have become vulnerable for even the most established organizations. Nonprofits must "get real" in their budgeting or suffer the consequences.

Nonprofits get real in many ways. Some build surpluses into budget projections as an antidote to the inevitable winds of change that will blow their way. Others adopt an income-based approach to both budgeting and spending. On the budgeting side, this means that their income projections include only sources and amounts that are *certain* or *reasonably certain*. The budget is balanced by decreasing expenses rather than trumping up income.

This is a tough process to adopt for nonprofits more accustomed to wishful optimism in budget development. Responsible money managers face their income realities as they prepare annual budgets, rather than scramble for solutions after the fact.

Income-Based Budgeting Worksheet

	Certain	Reasonably Certain	Uncertain/ Possible	Total
SUPPORT				
Government Grants				
1. _____	$ _____	$ _____	$ _____	$ _____
2. _____	_____	_____	_____	_____
3. _____	_____	_____	_____	_____
Foundation Grants				
1. _____	_____	_____	_____	_____
2. _____	_____	_____	_____	_____
3. _____	_____	_____	_____	_____
4. _____	_____	_____	_____	_____
5. _____	_____	_____	_____	_____
6. _____	_____	_____	_____	_____
7. _____	_____	_____	_____	_____
8. _____	_____	_____	_____	_____
9. _____	_____	_____	_____	_____
Individual Contributions	_____	_____	_____	_____
In-Kind Support	_____	_____	_____	_____
Other				
1. _____	_____	_____	_____	_____
2. _____	_____	_____	_____	_____
3. _____	_____	_____	_____	_____
REVENUE				
Contracts				
1. _____	_____	_____	_____	_____
2. _____	_____	_____	_____	_____
3. _____	_____	_____	_____	_____
Earned Income				
1. _____	_____	_____	_____	_____
2. _____	_____	_____	_____	_____
3. _____	_____	_____	_____	_____
Membership Fee	_____	_____	_____	_____
Interest	_____	_____	_____	_____
Total Support and Revenue	$ _____	$ _____	$ _____	$ _____

Determining Your Financial Worth

When it comes to financial performance, the accounting industry gives us the *balance sheet* as a simple way to measure whether a nonprofit is gaining or losing ground from year to year. In one concise statement, the balance sheet tells you and your financial partners what your organization is worth at a date in time.

The balance sheet is comprised of three main sections: (1) Assets—what you own, (2) Liabilities—what you owe, and (3) Net Assets—what you're worth. The accounting equation that gives the balance sheet its title is:

Assets = Liabilities + Net Assets

Assets include cash, accounts receivable, grants receivable, inventory, prepaid expenses, real estate, property, and equipment. Assets are classified as *current* or *noncurrent*, separating those accounts that can be expected to turn into cash within the next year (current) from others. Noncurrent assets include fixed assets such as property and equipment, investments, and grants promised but scheduled to be received two or more years into the future.

Liabilities include accounts payable, accrued salaries and payroll taxes, notes and loans payable, and long term debts. Similar to assets, liabilities are classified as current (those obligations due within the year) and noncurrent (debts due beyond one year).

Net assets are the difference between what you own and what you owe. Net assets represent the accumulation of surpluses and deficits you've achieved since your organization began. If throughout the years your surpluses have exceeded your deficits, net assets will be positive. If the opposite is true, you'll show a negative net worth.

Most of us remember the *fund accounting* days when nonprofits weren't supposed to be worth anything. The Financial Accounting Standards Board's (FASB) re-look at how the nonprofit industry presents and classifies contributions infused new guidelines and language into the nonprofit lexicon in the mid-1990s.

Balance Sheet

------- December 31, __(year)__ -------

	Unrestricted	Temporarily Restricted	Total
ASSETS			
Current Assets			
Cash and Cash Equivalents	$ 13,000	$ 53,000	$ 66,000
Accounts Receivable	13,000	-0-	13,000
Contributions Receivable	-0-	47,000	47,000
Total Current Assets	$ 26,000	$100,000	$126,000
Property, Plant & Equip. (net)	40,000	-0-	40,000
Total Assets	$ 66,000	$100,000	$166,000
LIABILITIES AND NET ASSETS			
Current Liabilities			
Accounts Payable	$ 25,900	$ -0-	$ 25,900
Payroll Taxes Accrued & Withheld	2,100	-0-	2,100
Accrued Salaries	8,000	-0-	8,000
Accrued Vacation Pay	11,000	-0-	11,000
Refundable Advance	-0-	30,000	30,000
Total Current Liabilities	$ 47,000	$ 30,000	$ 77,000
Net Assets	19,000	70,000	89,000
Total Liabilities and Net Assets	$ 66,000	$100,000	$166,000

These standards, promulgated in Statements of Financial Accounting Standards (SFAS) #116 and #117, contain numerous technical mandates related to accounting for donations and contributions and subsequent financial statement presentation. On a more fundamental level, however, they represent a subtle but important shift in the importance of nonprofit net worth.

For years, the nonprofit industry relied on fund accounting to capture and describe a nonprofit's financial health. FASB's nonprofit accounting revisions replaced the term "fund balance" with "net assets." Although derived from the same equation, *net assets* implies that *assets should be greater than liabilities*. This is a subtle but fundamental shift away from the more passive and benign fund balance mentality most nonprofits grew up with.

In addition to the change from "fund balance" to "net assets," FASB's new accounting standards reclassified nonprofits' contributed assets. In place of operating, plant, and endowment funds, accountants now classify nonprofit assets as unrestricted, temporarily restricted, and permanently restricted.

Unrestricted net assets are free of any donor restrictions. *Temporarily restricted* net assets have donor-imposed limitations removed by action and/or time. *Permanently restricted* net assets contain donor-imposed requirements that may never be removed by either time or action.

Note that FASB's net asset classifications apply only to donor contributions. Earned revenues, most government grants and contracts, or any activity for which there was a "reciprocal exchange" are classified as unrestricted.

With this in mind, what clues can the balance sheet provide about your nonprofit's financial health?

Are your organization's assets greater than its liabilities? If so, your net asset position will be positive and shown without (parenthesis). If negative, then you're in a deficit position. In an economy with little slack, most nonprofits can't afford the luxury of annual or accumulated deficits.

Do you have enough cash to pay for current liabilities? Healthy organizations have enough cash in savings, checking, and collectable receivables to cover each dollar of outstanding current liabilities (bills due now but as yet unpaid).

Are you building rich but cash poor? Buildings, inventory, and uncollected receivables are important assets, but they don't pay the bills.

Do you have a payroll tax problem? If so, it will show up under the liabilities section of your balance sheet. Failure to pay payroll taxes is the easiest, but most dangerous, place for a nonprofit to fall behind. The IRS has a mission to collect tax revenues—and that includes your current and future grant income, whether restricted or not.

Have you received funds that are meant for future activities? If so, they'll be noted in the liabilities section as either "deferred revenue" or "refundable advance." Both terms refer to earned or contributed funds that you've received but must return if your organization cannot perform either the contract or the grant. Large deferred revenues without corresponding cash assets are a sure sign that to make ends meet, you're robbing Peter to pay Paul.

Tracking Income and Expense

The income statement (or "statement of activities," as SFAS #117 recaptioned it) provides another indicator of your nonprofit's financial fitness. As the balance sheet summarizes your net worth at a given point in time, the income statement tells you, your board, and your financial partners where your organization's income came from, where it went, and how much was left once expenses were subtracted from income.

Here's what else you can learn from this statement.

Did your annual income cover your organization's expenses? This is not a trick question; however, the answer may fool you. FASB's new accounting standards require that you recognize all *unconditional* grants and pledges as income in the year the grant or pledge is made.

Income Statement

-------- December 31, __(year)__ --------

	Unrestricted	Temporarily Restricted	Total
REVENUES, GAINS AND OTHER SUPPORT			
Contributions	$ 48,000	$ 120,000	$ 168,000
In-kind Contributions	10,000	-0-	10,000
Government Grants	400,000	-0-	400,000
Interest Income	300	-0-	300
Other	4,000	-0-	4,000
Net Assets Released from Restrictions	50,000	(50,000)	-0-
Total Revenue	**$ 512,300**	**$ 70,000**	**$582,300**
EXPENSES AND LOSSES			
Program A	$ 81,000	$ -0-	$ 81,000
Program B	30,300	-0-	30,300
Program C	154,000	-0-	154,000
Program D	142,000	-0-	142,000
Total Program Expenses	$407,300	$ -0-	$407,300
Management & General	99,200	-0-	99,200
Fundraising	10,200	-0-	10,200
Total Expenses and Losses	**$ 516,700**	**$ -0-**	**$ 516,700**
Change in Net Assets	$ (4,400)	$ 70,000	$ 65,600
Net Assets Beginning-of-Year	$ 23,400	$ -0-	$ 23,400
Net Assets End-of-Year	$ 19,000	$ 70,000	$ 89,000

Conditional grants or pledges are not required to be recorded. This means that if a foundation or other donor has awarded you a multi-year grant of $75,000 to be paid over three years, the entire amount must be recognized as income in the year the pledge is made, even though the balance of funds will be paid out over future years.

This new rule about income recognition may lead you or your financial partners to believe your organization has more money than it really has. To get a true picture of your *annual* income and expenses, read the "unrestricted" column or category only. For the most part, *future* income will be classified as "temporarily restricted."

What is your organization's money mix? Nonprofit income falls into two general types: *support* (contributions) and *revenue* (contract or fee income). Understanding your organization's income mix is more important than ever as government funding shrinks and nonprofits must either replace it with earned revenues, find other contributors, or cut their own budgets accordingly. At least once a year take a good hard look at how much of your income is support vs. revenue. How much is government vs. private? Can this mix be maintained in the future? Is it the right mix or should you be looking to other sectors for future income?

If your income statement shows a deficit in the unrestricted category— you'll know it by the (parenthesis)—how did it occur? Don't get confused by the new FASB language which replaces "surplus" and "deficit" with the phrase "change in net assets." It's still the same concept. Your organization either did or did not have enough money to meet its operating expenses. If it didn't, what is the plan to reverse this next year? Here there are only two choices—cut expenses or increase revenues.

What in-kind support did you receive from the community? In-kind support is an important indicator of the value your community places on your organization. As cash assets get tighter, volunteer labor and donated goods will become a larger part of the nonprofit financial equation.

What percentage of total expenses was spent on program, administrative, and fundraising activities? FASB now requires nonprofits to bundle these types of expenses into three explicit categories to make it easier for donors to track. However, the old rule of thumb still applies—program expenses should represent at least 70 percent of your total expense.

Financial Analysis Techniques

Using the balance sheet and income statement, nonprofit managers can develop key financial indicators of their worth and performance. Ratio analysis, for instance, provides several measurements of balance sheet and income statement performance. A few of the more general ratios are presented below. Your accountant or other financial professional can help you develop others that may be more specific to your business.

Current ratio divides your current assets (those assets that are expected to become cash within the next 12 months), by current liabilities (obligations due within the year). Here you're looking for a ratio of 1 or more to show that you have enough liquid assets to cover current obligations.

Current Assets/Current Liabilities = Current Ratio

Quick ratio also measures liquidity, but only the current assets that can quickly be turned to cash. The result is a more conservative measurement of your ability to pay current obligations.

Cash + Accounts Receivable/Current Liabilities = Quick Ratio

Cash on Hand to Current Liabilities ratio is an even more conservative indicator of your ability to pay current obligations. This ratio measures your liquidity strictly on the basis of cash on hand.

Cash/Current Liabilities = Cash on Hand to Current Liabilities Ratio

Debt to Net Assets ratio indicates how much of your net worth is comprised of debt. The higher the percentage, the more your organization relies on borrowed money for its ongoing operations.

Loans + Notes Payable/Net Assets = Debt to Net Assets Ratio

Monthly Information Every Nonprofit Board Needs to Know

	Month Ending	Year to Date
INCOME		
Contributions	_____	_____
Government Grants	_____	_____
Earned Income	_____	_____
Interest	_____	_____
Other	_____	_____
Subtotal	_____	_____
Carryover (+/-) from Previous Year	_____	_____
TOTAL INCOME	_____	_____
EXPENSES		
Personnel Costs	_____	_____
Health Insurance	_____	_____
FICA, Federal & State Taxes	_____	_____
Rent	_____	_____
All Other Expenses	_____	_____
TOTAL EXPENSES	_____	_____
Surplus/(Deficit)	_____	_____

OTHER INFORMATION

1. Uncollected receivables

   Over 30 days _____ Over 60 days _____

   Over 90 days _____ Over 120 days _____

2. Checking balance _____ Savings balance _____

3. Total budgeted income this year _____ % to date _____

4. Total budgeted expenses this year _____ % to date _____

5. Listing of this month's contributors:

   _____

   _____

   _____

   _____

6. Explanation of unusual expenses this month:

   _____

   _____

Contributions to Total Revenue ratio measures the percentage of your nonprofit's revenue that comes from contributed income. While there is no hard and fast rule here, you should ideally have a diverse mix of income sources. Even if more of your income is contributed than not, you should at least have a wide variety of contribution sources. In other words, don't have all of your eggs in one basket!

Contributed Income/Total Revenue = Contributions to Total Revenue Ratio

Program to Total Expenses ratio looks at how much of your expenses are used to support programming vs. how much is spent for general management and fundraising. A rule of thumb to follow is that at least 70 percent of your total expenses should be used to support programs. The higher this percentage, the better.

Program Services Expenses/Total Operating Expenses =
Program to Total Expenses Ratio

Tracking the Trends

Information from the balance sheet and income statement can also be used to create a financial trend line that tracks your organizational progress throughout the years. This is the type of information most boards of directors will want to monitor to ensure the organization's ability to perform and continue its mission.

Trend analysis in spreadsheet format displays your organization's operating income and expenses for a period of five years or more. Ultimately, this analysis measures positive or negative changes in your net asset position.

Nonprofit money managers interested in assessing their own financial worth will find it worth their time to go back to prior years' audits to pull this information together. This is the type of information that your board and financial partners will find invaluable.

Five-Year Financial Trend Line

	Current Year	Last Year			
Support & Revenue	$	$	$	$	$
Expenses	$	$	$	$	$
Change in Net Assets	$	$	$	$	$
Net Assets Beginning-of-Year	$	$	$	$	$
Net Assets End-of-Year	$	$	$	$	$

Explanation for positive or negative occurrences:

_____

_____

_____

_____

Presenting Your Worth to Financial Partners

Until now, we have focused on financial statements from your internal perspective as a manager or board member. Nonprofits must also report their financial condition to a variety of external financial investors who require an objective verification of financial statement reliability.

Audits—Your audit presents an independent, objective opinion as to the accuracy and credibility of your financial statements. The necessity of having an audit performed will depend on many factors: the state in which your organization is incorporated; your total revenues; the amount of contributions you receive each year; and specific sources of funds (for example, contracts for which you receive federal funding).

Audits issue an opinion on your balance sheet and income statement activities and provide a historical perspective on the sources and uses of your organization's cash for the period reported. The audit also contains a section of notes to support financial statement numbers and a statement of functional expense, which breaks down for you and the reader the distribution of expenses by program, administrative, and fundraising activities.

An audit also contains an opening letter from your accounting firm commenting on the overall reliability of their opinion. An *unqualified opinion* is a clean audit. That's what you're shooting for. Anything else (*qualified opinion* or *no-opinion*) should raise a red flag to you and your board about your agency's financial practices and/or position. In rare cases, auditors issue a "going concern" warning in their opinion letter. This is not done lightly and always spells grave concern about an organization's ability to continue in its current financial condition.

Management Letters—In addition to audited financial statements, your auditor will prepare a management letter for the board of directors commenting on your internal operations. These letters are sometimes prepared routinely; in other cases, particularly when there are no substantial irregularities to note, your board may have to ask for this letter.

Many boards and managers find that the management letter makes a valuable contribution to understanding their organization's accounting and internal control practices. Because the management letter is an

---

Audit Preparation Checklist (✓)

Documents
____ Minutes of committee and board of
     directors meetings
____ Grant and contract proposals and
     award letters
____ Lease agreements
____ Payroll-related forms and reports
____ Insurance policies
____ Loans and notes payable
____ Invoices and any correspondence
     from your nonprofit's attorney(s)

Financial Records
____ Bank statements and bank
     reconciliations for all cash and
     investment accounts
____ Year-to-date general ledger
____ Financial statements and trial
     balance for the end of the period
     being audited
____ Ledgers, journals and registers
____ Vendor invoices

Work Papers

For Operating Revenues:
____ Detailed listing of accounts
     receivable at year-end
____ Schedule of allowance for doubtful
     accounts with an explanation of how
     these amounts were arrived at
____ Depreciation schedule

For Liabilities, Including Salaries:
____ Detailed listing of accounts payable
     at year-end
____ Detailed listing of any loans and
     notes payable at year-end, with
     computations for any accrued
     interest and a schedule of future
     loan payments
____ Schedule of salaries payable at
     year-end
____ Schedule of payroll taxes and
     employee benefits payable at year-
     end
____ Schedule of year-to-date salaries
     and payroll taxes
____ Detailed schedule of employee
     vacation earned but not used as of
     year-end

____ Schedule of temporarily restricted
     contributions at year-end (in the
     past, this might have been
     considered deferred revenue)

For General Expenses:
____ Schedule of professional fees
     (i.e., amounts paid to attorneys,
     accountants and consultants)
____ Schedule of rent expense for the
     year
____ Listing of supplies and equipment
     costing more than $300

For Contributions:
____ Detailed listing of grants and
     contributions receivable
____ Recap of in-kind contributions
     received during the year

Miscellaneous:
____ Other schedules as requested by
     your auditor:

     _____
     _____
     _____

Keeping the Books: Developing Financial Capacity in Your Nonprofit Press
Copyright © 1996, 1997 The Stevens Group, Inc. All Rights Reserved.

internal document, nonprofits are under no obligation to provide this letter to funding or financial partners. You may do so, of course, but you are not obliged.

Your internal financial statements, the audit, and your financial trend line are the three most important financial tools you have as a nonprofit money manager. Understanding them inside and out will help you troubleshoot through financial downturns and analyze future opportunities from a position of knowledge and confidence.

Equally important, your sound financial understanding—coupled with a willingness to make course corrections as needed—will earn you a reputation as a smart money manager who both acts and behaves as if nonprofits counted.

▼

GETTING YOUR MONEY'S WORTH FROM YOUR LOCAL BANK

On the surface you might say that banks and nonprofits have little in common. Look beyond their profit and not-for-profit business motivations, however, and you'll find many similarities. Nonprofits and banks both provide valuable community services rooted in public trust and accountability. Just as important, both need to attract new money and maximize the assets they already have to operate as viable community entities.

Historically, nonprofits and banks have not been natural allies. True, community banks encourage their executives to become board members of local nonprofits, and many provide financial and in-kind support to nonprofits during annual fund drives. Few nonprofits do not have some form of checking or savings account relationship with their local bank or other financial institution.

But when it comes right down to it, neither the banking industry nor the nonprofit sector has tapped the enormous potential and value each has to the other. With the advent of the Community Reinvestment Act (CRA), civic banking, and other efforts to make funds and services available on a local level, some banks have reached out on a larger scale to nonprofits in their communities. Nonetheless, only the most savvy bankers see nonprofits as viable business contacts.

Smart nonprofit money managers learn to use their local bank as an active financial partner, an important resource to make the most of scarce assets.

It All Starts With a Handshake

From the outside, banks may seem like large, impersonal corporations. But the truth is, even in an age of technology, cultivating a relationship with your banker is the single most important step you can take to ensure that your nonprofit organization is making the most of its assets and able to obtain credit on a timely basis.

The first step toward relationship banking is to find a bank where your nonprofit is understood and valued for the service you're providing to the community. Although banks may reach out to you in the way of direct mail, billboards, and low-interest credit card promos, it is important to find a bank where someone "knows your name" and with whom you can have a long, steady working relationship.

There are many practical considerations to keep in mind as you choose a financial institution. The size of a bank is one of the first factors that many nonprofits evaluate.

Small Banks vs. Large Banks

Nonprofits frequently voice a certain skepticism that big banks and nonprofits don't mix. Some nonprofits have been burned by bigger banks whose loan authority and other key decisions are centralized in far-away headquarters or left to downtown number-crunchers who know nothing about the nonprofit or its community. Nonprofits in large urban areas get equally frustrated with big banks' tendency to rotate their bankers from place to place, right after the nonprofit "trains them in." Clearly this doesn't qualify as "relationship" banking!

It's been a little more than two decades since New York State ushered in the era of bank deregulation. Much to the outcry of the state's independent banks, the New York state legislature abolished the banking districts that had previously made it difficult for Manhattan's mega-banks to move upstate. Deregulation opened the landscape of smaller communities to such financial giants as Chase Manhattan, Citibank, and Chemical Bank.

Since then, the banking industry—once dominated at least in number by family-owned and operated independent banks—has undergone reeling changes the likes of which are almost unparalleled in any other industry.

Over the last 20 years, big banks have gotten bigger. Several small community banks have held their own, though certainly not without a struggle.

Big banks have a place in the nonprofit marketplace. They can offer services (or "products," as they call them) that a smaller bank can't provide. Large nonprofits whose financial requirements include multi-million dollar lines of credit, international currency, and trust-related endowment services belong in a large bank.

Can big banks offer a relationship approach? You bet they can, and many do. The new wave of "personal bankers" and "customer service representatives" is one way larger banks are competing with their smaller bank counterparts to attract customers seeking a one-stop banking experience. But big banks make their money on volume, and small and mid-size nonprofits operate at a scale that is often inconsistent with a larger bank's targeted market. Larger banks may still reach out to smaller nonprofits as part of their community mission, but in a relationship there are two sides to the equation—two equal sides.

Banking is no place for a nonprofit to be a second class citizen. In all too many financial transactions, particularly with private and public funders, nonprofits are cast into the role of supplicant. True relationships are interdependent. Each party has something the other needs. In a banking relationship, even when negotiating a loan, your nonprofit is a customer. That's how the bank should—and most assuredly will—treat you if you hold up your part of the bargain and leave the *poor me* attitude at the door.

But many nonprofits have learned their fundraising lines too well to get off their knees and back on their feet. Bankers, large or small, don't understand supplicancy. If you happen upon one in your pursuit for the right bank, walk the other way. You're a customer, worthy in your own right.

When all is said and done, the decision about where a nonprofit banks will come down to many factors that are less about a bank's size and more about finding a bank that keeps an eye on service, shows loyalty to you as a customer, and is willing to take an occasional risk on customers whose names and circumstances it knows well.

Selecting the Right Bank for You

There are many practical considerations that go into selecting a bank. Like everything else, making the right selection will be dictated by knowing what you're looking for. When shopping for a bank, jot down the type of services your organization currently requires and will need into the future. Note also the rates of interest you currently pay on loans or receive on deposited funds. Armed with these considerations as your starting point, here are eight tips for selecting the right bank for you.

Convenience—With the popularity of ATMs, bank by mail, phone and on-line services, a bank's location and hours may not be as important as they used to be. But for nonprofits with significant daily cash deposits, convenience is still the name of the game.

Size—As with any service provider, the larger your account, the more service and recognition you will get. The rule of thumb here is to find a bank that is large enough to grow with you, yet of a scale that you are considered a big or valuable account. The size of your account is determined by totaling all the funds you deposit in one year. You can be a million dollar customer account even if at this moment your bank balance is $2,000.

Products and Services—Are the bank's routine services consistent with the requirements of your nonprofit? How would the bank describe its ideal customer? Will the bank negotiate rates based on customer volume? Are loan and credit decisions made by the banker, a local committee, or are they made in a different location? These are among the many questions you'll want to know about the bank's services.

Cost per Transaction—What will it cost to bank there? Even the smallest banks offer a variety of products, each with its own fee structure. If you've been used to free checking and savings services because you're a nonprofit, don't count on this service for long. In most parts of the country, free services for nonprofits are becoming a thing of the past.

Lending Practices—If loans are part of your banking requirements, ask questions about the bank's lending practices. Who has what authority? What types of loans are taken to a loan committee? Is there a size limitation on loans reviewed by the credit officer? How much lead time is required to process a loan?

Negotiated Transactions—How does the bank price a "package" of services for an account of your size? Does it negotiate loan interest rates for its checking and savings customers, or do they receive the same interest rate as a non-depository customer? Are you able to negotiate items such as the terms and interest rates on certificates of deposit; service fees on checking accounts; minimum balance requirements; fees on credit cards; use of safe-deposit boxes; and overdraft protection?

CRA and Regulatory Compliance—Is the bank under scrutiny from federal regulators for either non-compliance with the Community Reinvestment Act (which evaluates the extent to which banks make funds available in low-income communities) or for regulatory improprieties? Throughout the late 1980s and early 1990s, the OCC (Office of the Comptroller of the Currency) and other regulators charged many banks with "unsafe and unsound" credit practices. Although most banks have since written off or worked out their troubled loans, you don't want to get caught in the wake of subsequent credit conservatism that became the norm of chastised banks.

Attitude Toward Nonprofits—Last, but certainly not least, is the bank's attitude toward your organization and toward nonprofits in general. You are a customer. Banks need customers. Be sure you are treated with the respect and consideration given to any business account of your size.

The Importance of Timing

We all know the value of good timing. Developing a good banking relationship is as dependent on timing as any of the other considerations mentioned above. Like any relationship, the better things go in the beginning, the more likely they are to remain strong into the future.

Timing doesn't play as critical a role for nonprofits which require fairly simple and straightforward banking services. But when your organization needs multiple bank products, or when loans or other credit

Five Banking Tips for Nonprofits

TIP #1
Shop for Your Bank

- Convenience
- Size
- Products and services
- Cost per transaction
- Lending practices
- Negotiated transaction
- CRA and regulatory compliance
- Attitude toward you and other nonprofits
  —Respect
  —Importance
  —Value

TIP #2
Know Your Banker Before You Need Him/Her

- Begin this process when agency is in its strongest cash position
- Establish a working relationship
- Keep informed on a regular basis
  —Press releases
  —Audit
  —Quarterly financials
  —Introduce to Board Chair
- Determine banker's authority—who does (s)he report to
- Consider having a banker on your Board
- Ask for recommendations on investing excess cash; state your expectations for bank's involvement

TIP #3
Know What is Important to the Bank

- Qualifications of management and structure
- Existence of proper accounting systems
- Trend of market demand and present level
- Maintenance of adequate insurance
- Minimum working capital
- Mortgaging of assets to other creditors (for loans)
- Confidence in your presentation

TIP #4
Know What to Present in a Financial Proposal

- Amount to be borrowed
- Date loan is needed
- Use of the loan
- Repayment schedule
- Planned cash source of repayment
- Alternative repayment source
- Collateral or guarantee

TIP #5
Know How to Present Yourself

- Service for a fee, not a favor
- Ask questions, don't be intimidated
- Remember, you are a customer and banks need customers

products are part of your financial requirements, then the timing of your approach to the bank—whether as a first time or ongoing customer—is critical. Here are three timing tips from veteran nonprofit bank customers.

Approach the bank from a position of strength. Whether you are shopping for a bank or looking for a loan, approach the bank when your organization is in its strongest cash position. When you have something to sell—rather than something to gain—you can explain the work of your organization, its economic impact on the community, the nature of your revenue sources, and what you will be looking for from the bank. The stronger your cash or asset position, the more attractive you will be to the bank—and the more confident you will feel in your approach.

Know your banker before you need a loan. Just as wise nonprofits cultivate foundation and donor relationships before asking them for money, smart nonprofit money managers cultivate their bankers in much the same way. Once again, the right time to approach the bank for a loan is when you don't need the money. (We'll talk more about this in chapter 6.) Understanding a nonprofit's financial situation can be very confusing for a lender when heard for the first time. Smart nonprofits get to the bank in anticipation of a loan, so they can get all the educating out of the way.

Keep the bank informed on an ongoing basis. At the beginning of your banking or borrowing relationship, provide the bank with information on your organization, including press releases, annual reports, and last year's audit. If your organization anticipates borrowing in the future, keep them apprised of your financial status by providing quarterly financial statements. All of these items will keep the bank up to speed on your organization's progress and make it easier for you to access services when you need them.

Basic Bank Products: Checking and Savings Accounts

At the very minimum, most nonprofits have a checking and savings account at a local bank. When selecting an account, choose one that will cost you the least in fees or earn you the most interest. For instance, even though some checking accounts earn interest, you may actually come out ahead with a checking account that does not earn interest but has lower total fees. You need to do your own calculations to see which option is most cost-effective for your organization.

Many accounts have a "minimum balance" requirement. Some banks calculate this amount on an average daily basis; others, on the lowest balance in the account during the month. Because the bank will charge a fee if your account falls below the minimum, find out how this amount is determined for your specific account. In some cases, the combined balances of your checking and savings accounts can be used to meet the minimum requirement. If you can't meet the minimum balance requirement, do not open that particular account. Instead, select one with the next best interest rate or the lowest total fees.

In addition to account maintenance fees, be aware of other fees that a bank may charge you. For example, you may be charged for each check that you write, checks that are returned, stop-payment orders, overdraft fees, and withdrawals from a non-bank ATM. In some instances, you may be able to negotiate these fees with your banker.

To open either a checking or savings account, you will need a corporate resolution from your board of directors. This resolution should include the date that the board met and approved the opening of a bank account, the authorization of certain officers to sign checks and borrow money, and the signature of the corporate secretary. Note that many banks will have a standard corporate resolution form for your use. The bank will also require signature cards from the individuals authorized to transact business on behalf of your organization. Whenever these individuals change, new signature cards must be obtained.

Reading Your Bank Statement

Banks send monthly statements on checking and savings accounts in either an individual or a consolidated format. Your bank statement will include all transactions made on the accounts—deposits, withdrawals, and checks written and cleared—up to a certain cut-off date. It will also include any interest paid and service charges you've incurred.

Your bank statement documents your monthly transactions from the bank's point of view. Your job is to make sure that the bank's version matches your own version of what has transpired. This process is known as reconciling your bank statement. You will need to reconcile your bank statement with two internal documents: your general ledger and your check register. Complete the reconciliation process as soon as your bank statement arrives each month.

Steps to Reconciling Your Bank Statement

STEP #1

Compare your bank statement to your check register. Note which checks, deposits, and withdrawals have cleared your account. Identify any outstanding transactions on a separate form (see Step 4).

STEP #2

Subtract from your general ledger cash account any service, miscellaneous, or automatic charges shown on the bank statement.

STEP #3

Add to your general ledger any interest earned as shown on your bank statement.

STEP #4

Complete a bank account reconciliation form:

• At the top of the form, list the account's ending balance as recorded by the bank.

• Add any deposits made after the ending date on the statement.

• Subtract any outstanding checks or withdrawals made after the ending date on the statement.

Bank Account Reconciliation Form

Bank Name: _____

Account Number: _____

Date of Statement: _____

Ending Balance Per Bank Statement $ _____

Add: Deposits not yet credited on statement

Date	Description	Amount

Total Additions (+) $_____

Subtract: Outstanding checks and withdrawals

Date	Check Number	Amount

Total Subtractions (−) $_____

Balance (should match general ledger cash account) = $ _____

Note that the final amount should agree with the balance in your general ledger cash account. But what happens when these two amounts do not match? Most mistakes reflect problems in one or more of the following areas:

— Adding or subtracting incorrectly.

— Posting the wrong dollar amounts in your check register.

— Failing to enter all interest and service charges on your general ledger.

— Failing to identify all outstanding checks, deposits, and withdrawals.

Bank errors can also occur, including errors in data entry or simple math errors. If you locate a bank error, document it in writing and notify the bank as soon as possible. The sooner you report any discrepancies to the bank, the more quickly they can be resolved. For normal account activity, most banks require that you report any problems within 30 days. Special provisions, including a reporting period of up to 60 days, apply if the difference involves a credit line transaction or an electronic funds transfer.

Availability of Funds—The available balance on your account is the amount you could withdraw if you were to close your account today. Availability reflects the time lag, or "float," between crediting an account with a deposit and the actual collection of funds. Only funds that have completed the processing cycle and are known to be good are available for withdrawal.

Banks are regulated by law as to the length of time they can "hold" deposits. Funds from local checks, state and local government checks, cashier's checks, certified checks, cash, and wire transfers must be available by the second business day following the day of deposit. Funds from nonlocal checks must be available by the fifth business day. Direct deposit must be made available on the day the bank receives them. The only items whose availability is up to the discretion of a bank are ATM deposits. By law, this collection period must be disclosed to you by the bank.

It is important to know the availability of funds to prevent overdrafts on your account. Availability of funds is an issue around which you can negotiate with your banker. If you have a long-standing relationship with the bank or have a strong credit rating, the bank may make your money available more quickly.

Using the Float—With an understanding of the availability of funds, you can also time your payments to keep money in your interest-bearing account as long as possible. For instance, transfer funds from your savings to your checking account the same day you write a check. Pay your bills when they are due, not before. These simple steps can help you maximize interest earnings and minimize expenses.

Be careful, however, when dealing with electronic transfers of funds. Automatic payments and transfers made by phone, ATMs, or on-line are immediate. There is no "float," or time lag, as there would be if you were writing a check.

Taking Care of Business With Technology

The first part of this chapter examined the importance of relationship banking. In this section, we look at how you can use banking technology to your advantage. Whether it's a matter of convenience, speed, or efficiency, technology can enhance your ability to manage your organization's financial resources and conduct its business.

Automated Teller Machines—In the past 15 years, automated teller machines (ATMs) have emerged as a handy, efficient—albeit impersonal—means to conduct certain bank transactions. They let you withdraw or deposit funds from a checking or savings account, make transfers between accounts, and obtain account information. ATMs offer convenience of location and are accessible 24 hours a day. ATMs that are part of a larger network, such as Plus or Cirrus, allow you to access funds and account information even if you are out of state.

Although ATM privileges come as a standard component of many checking account packages, nonprofits should use them with extreme discretion.

For instance, your bank can limit access to account information to certain staff or prevent any withdrawals from ATMs. The more closely you guard your ATM access, the less likely misuse or fraud will occur.

Make sure to record every ATM transaction and keep receipts to verify them with your bank statement. In the case of deposits, banks consider ATM receipts provisional until they have been confirmed by the bank personnel who post your deposit or payment. Also, banks have different policies on "holding" checks deposited at an ATM. It may be several working days before your deposit is considered available for withdrawal.

Electronic Banking—In some areas, nonprofits can conduct "electronic banking" on the phone and by personal computers ("on-line banking"). The only requirement for banking by phone is a touch-tone phone and, for account transactions, a security code. In contrast, on-line banking requires a personal computer, modem, and communication software package. Note that many banks do not charge for banking by phone. However, most banks charge an additional monthly fee for on-line banking.

For any type of electronic banking, maintain a record of all your transactions, including the date, time, and amount of transaction. For on-line banking, print out hard copies of all your computer transactions. Reconcile your monthly activity against your bank statement as soon as it arrives. If any discrepancies arise, you should document the situation in writing and notify the bank immediately.

Credit Cards—Most banks offer Visa, MasterCard, or other major credit card accounts. Your organization may find it helpful to obtain a credit card, especially for items such as business travel and ordering supplies or publications that require pre-payment. We recommend that you use a credit card only as a convenient form of payment. When used as a financing mechanism, credit cards are simply too expensive. Other options—such as a loan or line of credit from a bank—will require more advance planning than "pulling out the plastic," but they will be a better use of your money in the long run.

When deciding which card to obtain, you should evaluate the card's annual fee, its annual percentage rate (APR), and if there is a grace period during which no interest will be charged. By law, lenders are required to disclose this information to you in writing at the time you receive an application. If you will not pay off your full account balance each month, pay close attention to the interest rate. Interest rates on credit cards can vary widely, reaching more than 21 percent per year.

Debit Cards—Debit cards—also called "check-debit-ATM cards"—are rapidly gaining in popularity. A debit card functions in two distinct ways: as an "electronic check," which immediately debits your checking account at the time of a purchase, and as an ATM card, which allows you to deposit or withdraw funds at an automated teller machine.

Many banks offer debit cards that carry the name of a major credit card company. These debit cards are accepted as a form of payment wherever that credit card company is accepted. Checks, on the other hand, may not be. While some banks do not charge for use of a debit card, others charge a monthly maintenance fee.

Wire Transfers—Wire transfers enable a bank to electronically move funds to and from another financial institution, resulting in immediate availability of funds for the recipient of the transfer. If you need to use this service to make a purchase or payment, you must know the account numbers of the recipient account.

Some banks have a minimum balance requirement for the amount of funds to be transferred. In addition to a direct service fee for sending a transfer, many banks also charge for incoming transfers.

Direct Deposits—Many banks offer a direct deposit service for your organization's payroll. Because the bank deposits payroll funds directly into bank accounts, your employees do not have to wait in line at the bank to deposit their checks. Moreover, their funds are available for withdrawal that same day.

Banks also accept direct deposit of other recurring payments, such as Social Security checks and retirement benefits. The service charge for direct deposit of payroll is usually charged to the employer.

Banking by Mail—While the U.S. Postal Service may not be considered a new technology, it is nonetheless a convenient way to conduct many of your banking transactions. To deposit checks into an account, endorse the check with the words "For Deposit Only," followed by your account number and signature. Complete a deposit slip and make a photocopy of it as well as both sides of the check. Request a deposit receipt from the bank and make sure to record the date you mailed the envelope.

You can also "bank by mail" to transfer funds, renew certificates of deposit, and order a stop payment. Call your banker and ask to have appropriate forms sent to you.

Note: Do not send cash through the mail. If lost, it is impossible to track or retrieve.

Technology allows you to conduct many bank transactions quickly, efficiently, and conveniently. However, you can also speed up even "old fashioned" ways of conducting bank business. For deposits, use a bank's night deposit box (and at any time of the day, as far as that goes!). Your deposit will be in a secured receptacle and will be posted by the start of the next business day. You can also try banking during off-hours, such as midmorning or midafternoon. In this way, you can avoid longer lines and conduct your business more quickly. Finally, when you call to make an appointment with a bank representative, ask to receive paperwork that you can complete ahead of time. In many cases, all you will need to do at the bank is sign the papers.

Bank Products That Make Your Life Easier

As competition in the financial services industry increases, the number and variety of bank products also increase. Today, a large bank may offer as many as 200 separate financial services and products. Following is a brief look at just a few of the services your local bank might offer.

Cash Management Services—If you have large deposits in a bank, you may benefit from various cash management services. A "sweep account," for instance, will take any balance over a specified minimum in an interest-free account and automatically "sweep" it each night into an interest-bearing investment pool. This gives you added earnings and, depending on the particular arrangement, added security through special FDIC protection or collateral provided by the bank.

401(k) Plans—Your bank can help you set up and administer a 401(k) plan as a retirement planning vehicle for your employees. Until recently, nonprofits had only the option of 403(b) plans. However, recent legislation now allows tax-exempt organizations to have 401(k) plans for plan years beginning after December 31, 1996. Employee contributions to their 401(k) are generally not included in their taxable income for that year. Moreover, earnings on the account are not taxed until they are distributed. As an employer, you can contribute to individual 401(k) plans through an employer "match."

Payroll Services—Your bank may offer a service to manage your payroll function, including calculating each employee's gross pay, making all required deductions, depositing net pay directly into employee accounts, providing detailed reports to you as the employer, and generating W-2 forms at year-end. Banks typically charge for payroll services based on the number of employees being paid.

Lockbox Service—A lockbox service authorizes a bank to rent a post-office box in your name to receive payments such as donations and memberships. If your organization receives a substantial number of payments through the mail, a lockbox service could significantly help reduce delays in receiving and depositing funds, thereby allowing you to earn higher amounts of interest. Also, many banks are able to process credit card and debit card payments. Banks will often charge on a per-item basis for a lockbox service in addition to a monthly fee.

There are many other ways in which a bank can help you make the most of your financial resources, including helping you set up and manage an endowment through its trust department, giving you investment advice, leasing equipment, or providing insurance products for your organization. Regardless of the specific service, your bank can be a significant partner in your financial picture. And the smarter you are in utilizing your available resources, the more you'll get your money's worth.

Choosing the right financial partner is an important step to becoming a smart money manager. This is especially true when it comes to cash management, the focus of the next chapter. Whether you have excess cash or not enough, it pays to know the right people at the right time. Your banker may not be the only "right person," but he or she is certainly one of them.

▼

MANAGING CASH FLOW

Several years ago, a television commercial featured a young, freckle-faced child with a ready-to-eat hamburger in one hand and a full but uncooperative bottle of ketchup in the other. With Carly Simon's "Anticipation" playing in the background, every viewer could relate to the child's frustrated wait for the stubborn ketchup to pour from the bottle.

In its most elemental form, this commercial serves up the perfect metaphor for understanding cash flow—a term that relates to time and means *having sufficient income when needed to meet expenses.* Just like the commercial's hamburger and uncooperative ketchup, nonprofits often find themselves with ready-to-be-paid expenses waiting for confirmed but delayed revenues.

When it comes to cash management, your job as a nonprofit manager is a little like weighting a teeter-totter. You need to anticipate, plan, and balance the flow of cash *into* your organization against the flow of cash *out of* your organization. Why? To enable you to have enough cash when you need it and to make the most of excess cash.

This chapter will introduce you to the ins and outs of cash management. The two chapters that follow explore how to make the most of excess cash (yes, this can and does happen among nonprofits!) and what to do when you don't have enough. First, however, let's look at the difference between *negative cash flow* and a *deficit,* a common point of confusion among nonprofits.

Defining Negative Cash Flow

Many nonprofits have trouble distinguishing cash flow problems from operating deficits. What's the difference?

Negative cash flow occurs when your demand for cash is higher than the amount of cash you have on hand—a situation that, although disruptive to smooth operations, shouldn't be confused with running a deficit. Negative cash flow assumes that, within the course of the year, there will be enough money to handle all budgeted financial obligations. The problem is that the receipt of funds will be slower than the time period in which bills must be paid. Like the slow-flowing bottle of ketchup, negative cash flow is a timing issue.

A *deficit* on the other hand, occurs when nonprofits overspend their operating income. Naturally, when organizations spend more annually than they receive, there will be cash flow problems. But in such cases, negative cash flow is a symptom of the deeper deficit problem. Here's an example of the difference.

The St. Lucas Home for Children operates with a budget of $500,000. Eighty-five percent of its income ($425,000) comes from government and United Way funds. The other 15 percent is raised annually from local foundations. Although the St. Lucas Home has a good fundraising track record, each year dollars seem more difficult to raise. Consequently, the executive director, unsure of how much grant support will be received, manages the agency within the $425,000 amount she is sure to receive.

When grants are ultimately awarded, additional program plans are implemented. However, at the start of the annual contract cycle each year, there is a predictable two-month delay in payment of government funds. This results in negative cash flow—a timing problem. Money is needed *now* to pay for expenses that will be reimbursed *later.*

A quick change of circumstances will demonstrate the difference between the negative cash flow situation described above and a deficit. Let's use the St. Lucas Home again, making the same assumptions about its budget size and income.

This time, instead of spending 85 percent of its income until there are firm grant commitments, St. Lucas Home spends at the full $500,000 budgeted level. If the agency is unable to raise an additional $75,000 of grant support during the course of the year, it will face negative cash flow somewhere along the line. However, the resulting cash shortfall is not a matter of timing, but rather a lack of adequate income. St. Lucas Home has spent more money than it will receive in income—and that spells deficit.

Anticipating Revenues and Expenses

Cash flow projections are an important management tool for nonprofits that experience ebbs and flows in income. Your goal in projecting cash flow is to accurately anticipate the sources and timing of cash income and to balance each against a projected schedule of disbursements. Unlike the budgeting or fundraising process—which often encourages an optimistic approach to income—cash flow projections take a hard, realistic look at when your income and expenses will come in and go out.

Cash flow projections answer the questions "When?" and "How much?" Accurate projections are important in anticipating cash flow. This is not the place for wishful thinking. Instead, it is your opportunity to take a hard look at the timing of potential receipts and disbursements with the goal of avoiding potential cash short falls. Here is where good record keeping pays off.

Historical data can tell you when certain payments have been made in the past, or when income has been received. In the absence of historical records, last year's check register can be used to re-create comparative receipt and disbursements patterns, adding in new expenses and income sources on a best-guess basis.

Projecting Cash Flow

To project your organization's cash flow, begin by listing confirmed budgeted income sources into the months you anticipate their receipt. Be conservative! If income has been promised for January but you know from experience that it will come in March, list it in the March column. This is also the time to think through whether certain funding comes in a lump sum or whether it is paid in installments.

Cash Flow Projections

	January	February	March	April	May	June
Cash Receipts						
County Contract	$ 75,000	$ 75,000	$ 75,000	$ 75,000	$ 75,000	$ 75,000
United Way	10,000	10,000	10,000	10,000	10,000	10,000
Special Event						15,000
Confirmed Grant	5,000					
Total Receipts	$ 90,000	$ 85,000	$ 85,000	$ 85,000	$ 85,000	$100,000
Cash Disbursements						
Payroll-Related	$ 70,000	$ 70,000	$ 70,000	$ 70,000	$ 70,000	$ 70,000
Rent	4,500	4,500	4,500	4,500	4,500	4,500
Utilities	800	800	800	600	500	500
Other Operating	5,200	5,200	5,500	4,900	5,800	3,700
Insurance/Audit				28,000		9,000
Special Event Expense					4,200	6,800
Total Disbursements	$ 80,500	$ 80,500	$ 80,800	$108,000	$ 85,000	$ 94,500
Cash Excess (short)	$ 9,500	$ 4,500	$ 4,200	$ (23,000)	$ -0-	$ 5,500
Beginning Cash Balance	800	10,300	14,800	19,000	(4,000)	(4,000)
Ending Cash Balance	$ 10,300	$ 14,800	$ 19,000	$ (4,000)	$ (4,000)	$ 1,500

Formula: Cash Receipts – Cash Disbursements + Beginning Cash Balance = Ending Cash Balance

From Funding to Financing
Copyright © 1988, 1997 The Stevens Group, Inc. All Rights Reserved.

To project expenses, first identify those budget items that occur monthly and whose amounts are constant. Divide these expenses by 12 and place them into each of the monthly expected expense columns. Place expenses that vary from month to month, or require one annual payment, in the month you anticipate their payment.

Having realistically determined the timing of income and expenses for each month, a series of calculations will tell you whether there will be sufficient cash in each month to meet expense requirements. But before putting pencil to paper (or setting up your formula in your computer spreadsheet file), add in the beginning cash balance—the amount of cash available at the beginning of the projection period. From there it is a series of steps in addition and subtraction. The formula looks like this:

Cash Receipts – Disbursements = Excess Cash (Shortfall)
+ Beginning Balance = Ending Cash Balance

Note that each month's ending cash balance becomes the following month's beginning balance. If the ending monthly balance is positive, there is enough money to meet that month's expenses without adjustment. If the ending monthly balance is negative, steps must be taken to increase that month's income or decrease its disbursements.

Remember that cash flow projections are internal documents done for your own benefit. They allow you to be alert and prepared for the reality and timing of your organization's projected income and expenses.

Payables and Receivables

Every nonprofit, irrespective of size, has bills to pay. Along with those bills, many nonprofits collect receivables, pledges, or fundraising proceeds from a variety of sources. Just like your small business counterparts, nonprofits need a good payables and receivables management system which tracks what you owe and what others owe you.

Few nonprofits would dispute that the goal of a good payables systems is to pay bills according to schedule. All too frequently, however, nonprofits

Seven Ways to Improve Cash Flow

1. Set up an "aging" system that separates outstanding invoices (receivables) by how long they've been overdue; i.e., 30, 60, 90, 120 days or longer.

2. Identify and contact slow-paying customers with a proposed game plan to accelerate payment.

3. Don't be embarrassed to pursue delinquent accounts.

4. If you rely on contracts or fees, establish a regular billing cycle and don't deviate from it. Too often the billing process gets put on the back burner. The shorter you are on cash, the higher should be the priority placed on your monthly billing process.

5. Explore taking payment via credit card. The attendant usage fee can be a small price to pay when the cost of collecting delinquent accounts is factored in.

6. Consider a collection agency if the age and amount of outstanding receivables warrants it.

7. Initiate a write-off policy when a receivable gets to be a certain age, or you have given up hope of collecting.

need to be convinced that the goal of their accounts receivable system is to collect what is owed to them in the shortest time possible. Some nonprofits are so service-oriented they forget they are in business. Meanwhile, they experience severe cash flow problems that threaten their organization's existence. Too often, if they could collect what is owed to them, their own cash problems would disappear.

On the payables side, your goal is to balance the amounts you owe with how much cash is available to spend. Certain bills carry the option to be paid over time. Where that option exists, nonprofits with chronic cash flow problems should take full advantage. From a credit standpoint, it is better to make partial payments on all bills than to pay some in full and nothing on others.

There are also times when there is sufficient cash to fully meet that month's expenses, but to do so would jeopardize the ability to make even minimum payments on next month's obligations. Here again, cash stability dictates that minimum payments be made in the first month, so that money can be saved for the following month's expenses. This is a difficult concept to grasp for those of us raised with the notion that bills must be paid in full and interest expense avoided at all costs.

One last word on payables and receivables. Many nonprofit managers leave all decisions about receivables, payables, credit, and collection policies to their business managers. In cash poor organizations, these should also be executive management decisions.

Too often, bookkeepers and accountants are the last people in the organization to know about certain management decisions that will put a strain on cash flow. They fulfill their obligation by paying the monthly bills, only to find out that management has recently contracted for a new brochure or an annual report, authorized a pay raise or out-of-town seminar for an employee, or in some other way obligated the organization's cash. Some managers find it hard to understand that just because "it's in the budget" doesn't mean there is cash available at that moment to cover all budgeted obligations. If your nonprofit tends to be short of cash, communicate with your financial staff before creating obligations. In that way you will avoid needless cash flow problems.

Planning Ahead

Sometimes, despite your best efforts at pursuing collections or limiting spending, you project that two months from now your organization will run short of cash.

When you find yourself in these circumstances, a short-term working capital loan or line of credit from the bank may be just what's needed for stabilizing cash flow. Smart nonprofit managers understand the benefits of an occasional cash flow loan to balance out revenue-timing problems. The more experienced managers also know that the time to approach the bank is now, when their organization is in a stronger cash position.

Bankers, like the rest of us, appreciate foresight. Your ability to anticipate upcoming cash flow needs will give the loan officer plenty of time to understand and process your loan request. Better yet, it will encourage the bank to see your potential loan request as part of a financing plan— something you anticipated—rather than a crisis that caught you off guard.

On the other hand, one of the side benefits of projecting monthly cash flow is that your organization will sometimes find itself in a positive cash position. When that happens, excess cash can become its own mini-profit center. Unless specifically prohibited by a funder, there is no reason why you can't put excess cash to use just as you would any other resource.

However, having excess cash is no time to let your "management guard" down. In fact, excess cash calls for the same amount of prudence and management as when you don't have enough cash. In these days of diminishing unrestricted income, a nonprofit foregoes $50 for every $1,000 sitting "idle" in a zero-interest checking account (assuming a 5 percent return). Accurate cash forecasts and active cash management can substantially increase your cash position.

Cash management is a critical tool for smart money managers. Before looking at steps to take when you don't have enough cash, let's further explore how you can maximize excess cash.

SMART SAVINGS: MAKING THE MOST OF YOUR EXCESS CASH

One of the questions nonprofits most frequently ask financial management consultants is "How can we establish an endowment?" When probed a little more, what they are really asking is "How can we generate an extra $10,000, $20,000 or $30,000 for our annual operating budget?" Faced with the definition of an *endowment*—a permanent investment, contributed by an outside donor, whose earnings alone are available for annual operations—most organizations agree that it's not an endowment they want. Rather, they're looking for unrestricted extra cash.

Endowments may not be for every nonprofit. But as a financial instrument, they legitimize two concepts that every nonprofit can use: savings and investing. On an individual level, we all know how important savings are to our financial future. No matter what our income or age level, most of us find ourselves saving for one goal or another. You'd be surprised, however, to find a college student saving for retirement or a retiree saving to buy a home. Likewise, the financial goals of nonprofits typically fall into a pattern consistent with their own financial life cycle.

Start-up nonprofits are generally *income focused*—it's tough to save when you can't make ends meet. Growing nonprofits need *cash reserves* to stem their cash flow and receivables problems. Established nonprofits are more frequently able to invest funds for a longer period of time, and for some, *endowments* are just what's needed to perpetuate their services over the long term.

This chapter is about smart savings techniques that go beyond your local bank's passbook savings accounts. As in other chapters, you can apply this chapter's philosophy and general advice no matter what your nonprofit size or shape. But just like the personal savings life cycle we mentioned above, we urge you to use your own good judgment when choosing one or another of the tips mentioned herein. For a nonprofit that consistently has trouble bringing in enough money to cover its operating expenses, it makes little sense to develop plans for a cash reserve or endowment. As in any other type of goal setting, you have to start with where you are, not where you wish you were.

Setting Financial Goals

Financial goals are an abstract way to think about your organization's overall financial needs. Most nonprofits don't have much trouble creating income and expense plans for their annual operating budgets. Too few, however, set overall financial goals that supersede a one-year time horizon—goals such as eradicating a $60,000 deficit over the next five years by bringing in an extra $12,000 a year in operating revenues, or saving $50,000 over the next three years to publish a commemorative "Twenty-Year Report."

If you're cash-strapped, these may seem to be unrealistic goals. But, if you buy into this book's fundamental premise—*the less you have, the more you need to make of it*—then financial goal setting is as much for you as for your more resource-healthy counterparts. Will it be painless? No. Saving money is never painless, no matter how much you have.

Setting and achieving financial goals is an important part of a nonprofit board's fiduciary responsibility. Goal setting starts with a thorough review of the financial condition of your organization. Most boards know how to take *defensive* measures to ensure that their organization is operating with fiscal prudence. With the help of their auditor or other outside financial professionals, they establish internal control procedures for record keeping, check signing, and other internal fiscal transactions.

But what's defense without offense? Fiduciary responsibility should prompt nonprofit boards to set overarching financial goals for their organizations as well—goals that are achievable and in the best interest of the overall financial health of the organization.

On the surface, it's hard to argue with this common sense advice. So what gets in the way of acting on this advice? The same thing that stops us from keeping our New Year's resolution or starting that new exercise program. When we begin to convert the plan into action, it hurts. The more it hurts, the easier it is to abandon.

Financial goal setting starts with at least a five-year look at certain organizational financial trends. The "Financial Trend Line" in chapter 2 is a good model to follow. This historical analysis will tell you whether you are gaining or losing organizational ground and provides a solid starting point for setting goals.

From there, the process may take different shapes and forms depending on your circumstances. The key thing to remember, especially if you are doing this for the first time, is that by definition financial goals are both tangible and intangible. They require your commitment—and commitment means you'll need to plan ahead, write down your plan, and begin to save accordingly.

Surpluses and Fundraising

Before examining the various savings tools at your disposal, let's side step into the question that many people have once they realize endowments aren't in their current financial picture: "Will having a surplus hurt our chances for fundraising?" The truthful answer is both yes and no.

Before explaining further, let's be clear that throughout this chapter, when we're talking about how to generate a surplus, we're not talking about surplus for surplus sake. Contrary to popular opinion, there is only so much money to go around in the nonprofit marketplace. Developing surpluses as a strategy for financial stability is one story. Hoarding your funds so they have no chance to benefit the community is another.

Will having a surplus hurt you as you set out to raise funds? There is still an ambivalence in the philanthropic community about surpluses. On the one hand, funders like the idea that nonprofits are behaving responsibly and have the internal capacity to create their own financial cushion. On the other hand, some funders use the existence of excess funds as a reason to deny a grant. *If they have their own funds, why do they need us?*

These funders are not criticizing you; they are affirming your good financial management! Nonetheless, this attitude can be a significant disincentive toward savings and general fiscal fitness.

Surpluses are even more difficult for government funders to deal with. Nonprofits on per-diem contracts with public entities often find their next year's contract cut by the value of their prior year's surplus. This happens even when annual financial performance exceeds that which was expected.

In the long run, surpluses are essential to your financial health, and smart nonprofits will plan for them accordingly. As dollars get tighter and more nonprofits clamor for the philanthropic dollar, contributors will invest in organizations that have a chance to be around awhile, not those who financially run on empty.

Understanding the Savings Sequence

Up until now, we've used the terms "surplus" and "savings" as generic catchalls to describe what to do with excess income. In reality, an actual sequence applies to how excess cash is generated and the types of savings instruments in which it is invested.

In broad terms, "surplus" refers to the cash remaining once annual expenses are subtracted from income. More specifically, however, the excess cash generated by nonprofits can be classified into four categories: interim funds, operating surplus, cash reserve, and endowment. Each of these is a legitimate tool for creating financially healthy nonprofits. Your own organizational life cycle will dictate which one of these tools is best for you now and in the future.

Interim Funds—You know how it feels to cash your payroll check and for at least a few minutes feel as if you've got money to spare? That's what interim funds are for a nonprofit. It's the cash you have in the bank right now, waiting to be spent on operating expenses. It may be excess for the moment, but it's not a surplus. Nonetheless, it's still a valuable commodity and worthy of some type of investment beyond earning minimal or no interest in your checking account.

Interim funds can be deceiving for nonprofits that don't understand their cash flow requirements. The presence of a hefty bank balance can trick you into thinking that there are no obligations against these funds. Be careful. One too many nonprofit could tell you its headaches over a snap decision made because there was "money in the bank" that was actually meant for a designated future activity.

Operating Surplus—This is the classic definition of surplus—you spent less last year than the income you brought in. There is money left over. Operating surpluses are generated in two ways: you plan them into the budget for the year or—through no foresight on your part—they just happen. Either way, you have an asset you didn't have at the beginning of the year. If you play your cards right, this asset can work *for* you rather than *against* you.

How might an operating surplus work against you? We've already mentioned the problems some nonprofits with surpluses encounter when raising funds from private or public funders. In the extreme, nonprofits generating mega-surpluses may fall under IRS scrutiny as well, but this generally happens only if these surpluses accumulate year after year and are never reinvested in mission-related activities.

How can a surplus work for you? There are three ways nonprofits generally put their surpluses to use: they spend them on an occasional or one-time expense; they save them for unexpected emergencies or opportunities; or they fritter the surplus away as happens to the best of us when we leave extra money sitting too long in our checkbooks!

If your financial plans call for developing annual surpluses as part of a long-term stabilization strategy, your board may want to establish a separate fund into which the surplus may be transferred periodically or at the end of the year. Once you or the board strategically sets these funds aside, your surplus becomes a cash or operating reserve.

Cash Reserve Funds—Surpluses that have been strategically set aside by management or board designation are known as reserve funds. Nonprofit reserves can take several forms. They can be "cash reserves" set aside to provide an internal line of credit for periodic cash shortfalls. They may be "operating reserves" designated for unexpected events, or "repair and replacement reserves," funded by building depreciation into the expense side of the operating budget that's designated for future building or equipment repairs.

For whatever purpose the reserve is created—and it can be all three—there is a common theme: *Reserves are planned; they don't just happen.* They are part of your savings offense. They won't happen unless you strategically think out your needs and your strategy, and then physically segregate these funds from the general operating account. Because of this, reserves are sometimes called "quasi-endowments" because they provide a certain amount of financial stability like an endowment. Unlike endowments, however, they are not permanent, and if self-generated, they are not considered restricted.

Reserve funds have one further advantage over a surplus: they provide a shield of protection for excess funds. The safest way to create this shield requires board involvement prior to the close of your fiscal year. If you have planned for, or otherwise foresee, closing the year with a surplus, have the board approve a motion to designate all or a portion of the surplus as a board-designated reserve, to be recorded on the audited balance sheet at fiscal year end. Provide these minutes to your auditor and have him or her set up a "board designated reserve fund" for general purposes or one of the purposes mentioned above, and there you have your shield.

Is this shield bullet proof? No. Will it ward off problems explaining unprotected surpluses? Yes. Does it demonstrate magnificent financial acumen and fiduciary responsibility on the part of your management and board of directors? Most definitely yes!

Endowments—Endowments are funds contributed to a nonprofit institution by outside supporters who stipulate that the principal value of their gift remain invested for perpetuity. Unless otherwise stated, the earnings from the investment may be used for operating purposes.

Endowments are neither created by nor managed like surpluses. In fact, they have nothing to do with a nonprofit's operating budget except for the once-a-year interest they generate for operations. Accounting standards require endowments to be set up in a separate fund outside the general account since they are permanently restricted.

Because the nonprofit financial vernacular is so imprecise when referring to extra cash, we take this opportunity to point out once again that the endowment's value to the operating budget is only by way of the earnings it produces off its corpus or principal investment.

Investment Options

Now that we've discussed the value of surplus and savings, let's look at the many investment options available through various financial institutions that will want your business once you have something to invest. For nonprofit managers not familiar with the world of investments, the options can be mind-boggling.

Your own circumstances will dictate which savings plan is right for you. Whether you have $500 or $500,000 to invest, you'll have two primary investment options: *cash instruments*—checking and savings accounts, money market investments, certificates of deposit, and Treasury bills; and *financial assets*—stock and bond funds. Knowing which of these investments is right for you will depend on your investment goals, your time horizon, and how much risk you can afford to take while staying within the bounds of fiscal prudence.

Speaking of prudence—for years nonprofits have taken the defensive approach to fiscal prudence, particularly when investing. Wary of losing their hard-won funds, many nonprofits venture no further than their local bank's passbook savings account, from which they receive maybe

2 percent interest. Passbook accounts are certainly preferable to keeping all your cash—interim funds and surpluses included—in a non-interest bearing checking account. But when choosing a savings vehicle for even their smallest investment, smart nonprofit managers take inflation into account. (Remember, the less you have, the more you need to make of it.) Smart savings doesn't mean you'll earn 15 or 20 percent on every investment. It does mean, however, that you earn the maximum amount possible for the amount of time and risk you can afford.

What's inflation? Inflation refers to an increase in the amount of money in circulation, resulting in a fall in its value and a rise in prices. In practical terms, inflation means that the dollars you save today will be worth less in the future than they are now. In the mid-1990s, inflation has hovered around 3 percent. This means that you need a return greater than 3 percent to have as much earning power the day you liquidate your investment as you did the day you put it in.

How about risk? How much risk can a prudent nonprofit afford to take with its funds? The concept of investment risk is not unlike taking any calculated risk in life. The first step is to know what you're getting into. The more you know about an investment product, the more you'll understand what you're doing.

The investment risk curve has two sides. On the one hand, you take the chance that your investment will sell at a lower price than what you originally paid for it. In that case, investing in stocks and real estate can be risky investments. On the other side, however, "safer" investment choices—such as bonds and cash instruments—run the risk that they won't keep pace with inflation.

Here is where the services of a financial consultant may come in handy. These professionals understand the history as well as the risk and reward of various investment products. Although some of us are closet "investment junkies," retaining a professional consultant or investment manager is a prudent idea, especially if you have significant permanent or long-term investments.

Although examining all the investment vehicles available to the nonprofit world is beyond the scope of this book, let's look at the overall range of possibilities most suited to the four types of savings instruments common in the nonprofit marketplace.

Cash Investments—This type of savings instrument is the appropriate choice for the interim funds or idle cash that you'll need within the next several months. In addition to passbook savings accounts, cash investments include money market investments and certificates of deposit (CDs), all available through your local bank. Money market investments and CDs typically offer a higher rate of return than passbook accounts.

Cash investments allow you to "park" your money on a temporary basis. That's their main advantage. They're also more liquid—that is, more quickly converted to cash—than the other savings vehicles we'll discuss, so you can generally get your money out faster and with less penalty than longer-term investment products. Certificates of deposit will have a time frame attached, however, so be sure your cash flow matches their time requirements.

Fixed-Income Investments—Although cash investments are technically considered fixed-income investments, most people are referring to *bond funds* when talking about this kind of savings instrument. When you buy a bond, you are loaning your money to a corporation, government, or local municipality with the guarantee that they'll repay your principal along with a "fixed" rate of return.

Sounds like a good deal, right? Bonds *can* be a very good investment for a nonprofit. They range from the ultra-safe U.S. Treasury Bills to the super risky junk bonds. Bond funds are influenced by time. The shorter the term, generally the safer the investment. But like any investment, an inverse correlation exists between safety and return. The safer the investment, the less it will pay.

Over the last two decades, bond funds have outperformed cash investments and have beaten inflation by several percentage points. They tend to be a good investment for your near-term or longer-term surpluses, cash reserve, or endowment funds—since they themselves come in the form of long-term, intermediate, and shorter-term instruments. Your investment advisor can help you choose the right fixed-income vehicle for you.

Equity Investments—This type of savings instrument allows you to invest in the stock of large and small corporations. Like bonds, some equity investments are riskier than others. Blue-chip, dividend paying stocks of "large cap" companies are the least risky equity instrument. The stock of "small cap," or smaller, companies falls on the other side of the risk scale.

Historically, stocks have outperformed bonds in terms of their investment yield. However, only nonprofits with endowments can generally afford to ride out the volatility that comes along with equity investments. If you need your cash out quickly, you don't want to be invested in the stock market.

Mutual Funds—With this type of savings instrument, your money is pooled with other investors into a professionally managed, mixed portfolio of stocks, bonds, and cash investments. The mix of the fund will depend on its investment objective, which can range from aggressive growth (the stocks of highly volatile small companies) to less risky municipal bond funds (bonds issued by state and local municipalities for public works projects).

Buying mutual funds may help you diversify your risk, but they don't relieve you of your responsibility to understand what you're getting into. Be sure to read the prospectus. If you don't understand it, ask your broker or call the company's representative. That's what they're there for.

Mutual funds are a popular investment tool for individual and nonprofit investors. Most nonprofits use mutual funds to hold their employees' 403(b) or 401(k) retirement funds, so they're among the more familiar investment vehicles for the industry. Mutual funds offer diversity and, depending on their investment strategy, they can also offer some degree of safety for your longer-term reserves and endowment assets.

One more thing about mutual funds: How and where you buy them will determine whether or not you'll pay a commission on the purchase. "No load" funds mean no commission will be charged, but watch out for hidden costs such as multiple fees and/or high operating costs.

There are many more things that can and should be said about investment management that are beyond our capabilities in this book. Remember that excellent investment advisors are available in every community to assist you with your investment decisions.

Our intent in this chapter is to get you thinking about where surplus, reserves, and endowments fit into your long-term financial goals. As a nonprofit, you have multiple savings and investment options that go well beyond traditional passbook and money market savings accounts. To make smart use of these savings options, set your financial goals and determine the amount you have to invest, the amount of time available until your cash will be needed, and the amount of risk you can take prudently.

Happy savings!

▼

GETTING CREDIT FOR WHAT YOU DO: HOW AND WHEN TO BORROW MONEY

For many nonprofits, the scene is all-too-familiar—there's a payroll to meet and the county's check has been delayed. Or perhaps the photocopier is on its last leg, or the agency needs additional space. Surprising as it may seem to some nonprofit managers, these are all valid reasons to borrow money.

Under the right circumstances, a loan will stabilize cash flow so your services are not jeopardized during cash-poor times. The ability to borrow money is often just what is needed to bring financial equilibrium to a nonprofit at the mercy of unpredictable income streams, growing service demands, or outdated equipment.

Borrowing Myths

Before we look at how, when, and why to borrow money, let's first clear up some of the most common myths that cause many nonprofits to shy away from taking out a loan.

Borrowing Puts Us in Debt. For some nonprofits, the term "borrow" is synonymous with debt—and since childhood we've learned that debt must be avoided. Stripped of its emotional baggage, however, debt is nothing more than a financial obligation. It is *temporary* money—money borrowed for a purpose and later repaid.

Every day, businesses, homeowners, car buyers, students, and nonprofits in need of immediate cash assume the obligation of debt, which they will later repay. True, some borrowers take on larger loans than they can handle and later find themselves in the type of "debt" that we would all do well to avoid. But prudent and responsible money managers quickly see the difference between using debt as a strategy and debt as a state of being.

No, Not Me! For some nonprofit managers, taking out a loan is a negative reflection on their money management skills. Yet many of the same people freely use credit cards—which are just another form of borrowing. Every time they charge a purchase, they enter into a debt transaction with the same interest and repayment obligations as a bank loan. Credit cards are nothing more than a convenient, user-friendly (and usually more costly!) source of borrowed cash.

Nonprofits Can't Afford Interest. Nonprofits frequently view loans as an expensive source of capital. But the carrying costs on a loan—be it for $10,000 or $100,000—are usually much less costly than the salary and expense it takes to generate the same dollar amount from foundation grants or government contracts.

Although nonprofits may wonder how they can afford the accompanying interest, there are actually several ways to cover the interest on a loan. For instance, you can build interest costs into the budget of a specific contract or into your fee structures. You can also use compensating bank deposits to lessen your interest rates, or you could obtain interest write-down assistance from an understanding funder. (From the funder's perspective, it is less costly to pay interest on a loan than make a grant in place of the loan.)

While we're on the subject, nobody likes to pay interest. We all try hard to avoid or minimize it. Nevertheless, in many situations, it may prove more costly to spend all of your organization's hard-earned cash up front than to use an installment alternative.

Borrowing Puts Nonprofits at Risk. Borrowing money creates a financial obligation. In this way, taking out a loan does put a nonprofit at risk. However, anytime your organization accepts a foundation grant or government contract, you also enter into an obligation that you must strictly honor. The only difference between the two obligations is that borrowed money has to be repaid.

The loan process creates a certain specificity that requires a borrower to anticipate the organization's financial activities over the life of the loan. The more specific you can be about future financial activities, the less at risk you and the lender will be.

Does this mean that any nonprofit that is able to project its financial future is an ideal candidate for a loan? Certainly not. Like any source of income, borrowed funds come with their share of strings attached. Be assured, however, that as much as banks and non-traditional lenders want to make loans, they'll never knowingly enter into a lending situation that puts them or you in financial jeopardy.

When a borrower defaults on a loan, the bank loses too. It gets back neither its original money nor the interest on the loan. And since bankers' salaries are paid in part from this interest, they literally have a vested interest in each borrower's success. The bank can't afford to knowingly put your organization at risk.

Knowing When to Borrow

Borrowing money is certainly not a suitable option for every nonprofit. But under the right circumstances, and when viewed without myth and stigma, *financing* a nonprofit's activities can be as viable as *funding* them.

Borrowing to Stabilize Cash Flow. Many nonprofits have felt the effect of the shift of federal and state dollars away from their programs. Some have been the recipients of start-up grant funding and now need stabilizing income to bridge the gap between the start-up phase of their project and the ongoing programmatic revenues.

Still other nonprofits, although they are appropriate grant candidates, have cash needs that do not coincide with a funder's grant timetable. Other nonprofits apply for loans when the timing of a grant payment puts a strain on their organization's cash flow. Nonprofits providing contractual services often need a line of credit, or a steady source of cash, to stabilize cash flow between billing and collection.

Borrowing for Capital Purchases. Nonprofits needing a new building, leasehold improvements, a new computer, phone system, or copy machine often struggle over where the purchase money will come from. Most look first to their own resources. Yet few nonprofit managers, even those with reserve funds, relish the prospect of depleting these funds that have taken so long to build.

One option is to apply for a grant. But often the timing and the cost involved in writing and waiting is more than the nonprofit can afford. The need exists *now* for a source of cash to make the capital purchase.

Many nonprofits find a loan to be just the right income source to handle these big-ticket items. Borrowing money for capital purchases provides an immediate source of cash which can then be repaid over time, usually with the flexibility of installment or lump sum payments.

Borrowing to Take Advantage of an Opportunity. "No finance, no romance!" This was the answer one social service agency gave when asked why it needed a loan. The agency had an opportunity to expand to another part of the state, a move that would diversify the organization's income and more than triple its budget. The board of directors saw this as an opportunity of a lifetime, one that fit within the agency's strategic mission.

There was only one hitch: Although the new venture would eventually provide a stable source of income, it required up-front money to get off the ground. Moreover, the agency needed several months' working capital until prior months' services could be billed and collected. There was no time for grant writing and the agency did not have enough savings to go ahead on its own. Financing made this opportunity possible.

Borrowing for Certain Emergencies. Unforeseen circumstances happen to the best of us. Grant proposals aren't funded, insurance or energy bills skyrocket unpredictably, boilers break, roofs leak, staff crises arise—all of which call for a quick source of cash. Nonprofits can sometimes use loans to handle these unanticipated situations.

Again, there's a hitch, one that applies to all borrowing: Every time you borrow money, you must know how, when, and from what source it will be repaid. This is the cardinal rule of borrowing. It presupposes your ability to project with accuracy the amount and timing of your organization's income and expenses, allowing enough room on the expense side to cover the agreed-upon loan repayment.

Does this sound impossible? Not if you know how to forecast cash flow. Many nonprofit managers have discovered that the better their ability to project their organization's income and expenses, the fewer emergency situations in which they will find themselves.

Determining the Type of Loan You Need

Although many types of loan products exist on the market, experience suggests that nonprofits borrow money for six specific purposes. These purposes dictate the type of loan that will best suit their financing needs. The following descriptions present a variety of loan types, along with the appropriate use and attendant risk of each.

Cash Flow and Bridge Loans—As the name suggests, cash flow loans bridge the gap between an immediate need for cash and a pending source of income. Cash flow and bridge loans always have a connected receivable, generally pledged as collateral for the loan. When the receivable is paid, the loan is repaid.

Cash flow and bridge loans are particularly useful for nonprofits without their own cash reserve funds. When county contract payments or foundation grants are delayed, when client fees are slow to be collected, or when income flows in an uneven pattern throughout the year, a bridge loan may be an ideal way to stabilize cash flow.

Cash flow and bridge loans are generally short-term and almost always repaid with 12 months. These type of loans are a good place to start the borrowing process because, in general, they pose the least risk both to the borrower and to the lender. The source of repayment is clearly identified, and often even the timing of payments can be predetermined. Yet even these loans are not without risk.

Every lender has made at least one loan in which the borrower's *sure* income unexpectedly dries up, taking with it not only the repayment source but also the collateral for the loan. That is why lenders often ask for an alternative source of repayment with a cash flow loan, in the event the "sure" receivable does not materialize.

Equipment Financing—Rather than spend hard-earned cash for a new copy machine, computer, phone system, or the like, many nonprofits choose instead to finance these purchases over a period of several months. Typically, the loan period for equipment financing will match or be somewhat less than the useful life of the asset.

Equipment financing is typically secured by the item being purchased. From a collateral perspective, this is ideal. The financed equipment provides a tangible piece of property that the bank can reclaim in the event of the borrower's default. But equipment purchases contribute new costs to the organization, usually without corresponding income. Thus, equipment financing carries the risk that debt service on the loan may not be repayable from the organization's monthly cash flow. Still, when it comes to equipment loans, good cash flow projections—along with collateral—usually will put a lender's mind at ease.

Capital Improvement Financing—Changing times often require non-profits to remodel or make physical improvements to their leased or owned facility. If your organization does not have cash reserves to handle these expenses, a loan may be a good alternative.

As with most other loans, a lender will first want to see cash flow information that demonstrates the ability of your organization to include the cost of these renovations in your operating budget over the life of the loan. Because most banks require collateral other than the improvements themselves, be prepared to pledge either cash or fixed assets when seeking a capital improvement loan.

Construction Loans and Mortgages—Banks make construction loans to erect new buildings or to add on to an existing structure. Construction loans carry a good deal of risk, the greatest of which is estimating how much the actual project will cost. Cost overruns are a fact of life in construction. First-time construction managers are often ill-equipped to make appropriate estimates and thus don't borrow enough money to pay contractors.

As with capital improvement financing, the loan officer will want to see cash flow projections for both the construction project itself and also for the operation of your organization. Loans made for new construction frequently are replaced or "taken out" by a mortgage. Mortgages are long-term loans made to acquire real property using the property itself as collateral.

Working Capital Loans—Many nonprofits—especially those experiencing rapid growth, significant inventory, or unpaid receivables—often find themselves short of cash. Their assets are not converting to cash quickly enough to meet current obligations. When this is true, the result is negative cash flow. Nonprofits can use working capital loans as a temporary solution to this type of problem.

Working capital loans take into account the full income potential of your organization. They are based on the entire working operations of your nonprofit. *Cash flow loans*, on the other hand, are tied to a specific receivable which can generally be identified and verified. Because cash flow loans are more specific and time limited, they are less risky than working capital loans.

Working capital loans are repaid from the general income stream of your organization. This presumes an overall positive financial condition, as well as some understanding of the cash flow history and projected trends of your agency.

Some working capital loans are made as lines of credit to cover seasonal or ongoing cash shortfalls. For example, a nonprofit art center may receive three quarters of its operating income in the last six months of the year. A line of credit—a loan approved up to a maximum amount to be drawn upon as needed—gives the organization the flexibility to borrow just what is needed to cover its monthly obligations. Interest is paid only on the portion of the line which is actually borrowed.

Lines of credit generally carry an annual retirement phase—a date upon which the loan needs to be repaid before renewing it for another year. This gives both the lender and the borrower some sense of security that the loan will not become an "evergreen credit." Bankers use this term to

---

Loan/Risk Chart

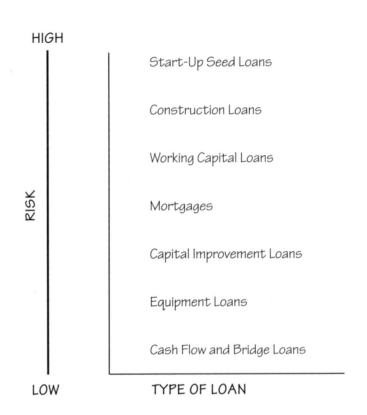

HIGH

Start-Up Seed Loans

Construction Loans

Working Capital Loans

RISK   Mortgages

Capital Improvement Loans

Equipment Loans

Cash Flow and Bridge Loans

LOW   TYPE OF LOAN

---

describe a line of credit that rolls over every time it is due because the borrower's financial condition has not yet allowed for repayment.

Working capital loans require both the borrower and the lender to have a good understanding of the nonprofit's current and future financial condition. Determining this takes time and patience on the part of both parties. But in these days of declining general operating support grants, working capital loans promise to play a much larger part in future income stabilization for many more nonprofits.

Start-Up Financing—Start-up financing, or seed capital, is the money that must be invested in a new nonprofit or program to move it from the idea stage into reality. Start-up funding usually takes the form of equity investments—contributions from foundations or private parties to get a new entity off the ground.

Sometimes, organizations unable to obtain start-up grants or support turn to the bank. Cases do exist where a start-up loan may be appropriate. However, without a track record or a secure income stream, it is difficult to obtain a loan for start-up capital. The primary risk for the lender is that the venture will never materialize, making the loan virtually unrecoverable. This ultimately would jeopardize the credit-worthiness of the borrower, and obtaining future financing would become difficult.

First-time borrowers, brand new organizations, and those generally unfamiliar with cash flow should not attempt to borrow money for seed capital. However, under the right circumstances, nonprofits with long and steady track records and experienced management may be appropriate candidates for start-up financing.

Getting the Loan

By the time most nonprofits get around to borrowing money, they have already become skilled at securing foundation grants, government contracts, and private contributions. They legitimately wonder if the approach that has made them successful fundraisers will serve them well in obtaining a loan. The five tips outlined below offer a short course in securing bank financing for would-be nonprofit borrowers.

Know When to Apply. As the old saying goes, "The only ones who can get a loan are those who don't need them!" Nonetheless, when applying for a loan, there is a substantial difference between those who have a critical business need and those who are desperate. Desperation carries an added risk for both the borrower and the lender—a risk that neither should take.

Seasoned borrowers know that the time to visit the bank is when they're in their best cash position. This demonstrates your ability to anticipate upcoming cash flow needs and gives both you and the loan officer adequate time to fully understand and process the loan request.

Yet there are times when cash flow problems or the need for quick cash sneak up on even the best prepared manager. In these circumstances, nonprofits with a firm understanding of their financial situation have a much better chance to negotiate a loan from a position of strength.

Bring the Right Financial Information. Nonprofits funded by foundations and government sources have traditionally operated with the budget as their primary financial document. Although the loan process does consider your organization's budget, it also requires close examination of several other financial documents that are not always analyzed in the grant process.

The *balance sheet* describes your organization's overall financial position at a given date in time and lists your organization's assets, liabilities, and net assets. Although nonprofits have often worried that a positive net asset position (fund balance) might undermine their ability to obtain a grant, the opposite is true for borrowing. The loan officer wants to see a positive fund balance—in other words, that your organization's assets exceed its liabilities. It is important that the balance sheet you present is current, and when unaudited, that it is accurate. (See chapter 2 for more on the balance sheet.)

The *income statement,* or statement of activities, for the prior year and most recent period tell a lender whether your nonprofit has lived within its means. These statements will be analyzed even more critically when current cash shortfalls might be attributed to last year's deficit. (See chapter 2 for more on the income statement.)

Cash flow projections showing anticipated income and expenses are also essential to the loan review process. They indicate how much money is needed over what period of time and how best the loan should be structured. They also forecast your organization's ability to have enough cash after the loan is repaid to carry on effectively. (See chapter 4 for more on cash flow.)

Educate the Lender. The loan officer is interested in more than just the financial condition of your organization. Your organization's mission and programs provide a necessary context within which the lender can judge the importance of the loan to your agency's purpose and stability. Be prepared to discuss the number of staff you employ, the market demand for your program, and how the community benefits from your services. Being able to explain these economic issues shows that you understand the relationship between your organization and the community or marketplace in which it exists.

This is also a good place to show your own dedication to the mission of your organization. Enthusiasm and dedication alone will not persuade the bank to make the loan. However, they do add credibility to your presentation and may even tip the scale positively in a marginal approval situation.

Demonstrate Management Capacity. Financial statements and cash forecasts lend themselves to an objective analysis. Assessing your management capacity—or "character," as the banking industry calls it— is much more subjective. You can make the job easier by knowing up front that the banker needs to make a judgment not only about your organization's ability to repay, but also about the likelihood that you, the manager, will repay.

Judging management strength is one of the most difficult functions a lender has to perform. Your knowledge of your organization's financial situation gives both you and the bank confidence in your presentation. Remember that your own attitude and demeanor play a major part in the lender's confidence in your application.

Know What to Present. The amount and purpose of the loan determines how extensive the financial application process will be. A complicated real-estate venture, a complex new program, or a project that has multiple partners will require a much more extensive review than a short-term cash flow loan. But in general, be prepared to address the following six points:

— *Amount to be borrowed*—Note that this is the first thing the loan officer will want to know. It pays to do both good budgeting and cash forecasting before going to the bank.

— *Date the loan is needed*—Advanced planning goes a long way toward enhancing your management credibility. It also gives the loan officer the necessary time to get the loan approved, prepare loan documents, get the check signed, and close the loan.

— *Use of the loan*—Be prepared to tell the banker the purpose of the loan.

— *Suggested repayment schedule*—There are many ways a loan can be structured for repayment. These include one lump-sum payment at the end of the loan period, interest only for a period of time, or monthly installment payments. Although some rules of thumb do exist, most banks will make every attempt to match the repayment schedule with an organization's cash flow. This is the surest way to guarantee that the loan will be repaid as promised.

— *Repayment source*—The more explicit and reliable the source of repayment, the more likely you are to get a loan. This is doubly true if you have an alternative source of repayment to offer in the event that the first falls through.

— *Collateral or guarantee*—Banks are under obligation with regulators to place safeguards, such as collateral, on loans. To protect their interests in the event of default, lenders usually expect you to pledge collateral in excess of the value of the loan.

Getting a loan is different from getting a grant. But it doesn't require any more time or any more skill than writing a grant or contract proposal. In fact, in most situations, the process of applying for and obtaining a loan takes far less time than that involved in traditional funding. You just need to know the rules and demonstrate your ability to repay.

Dealing With Denial

The reality of loan denial is all too common in the nonprofit sector. Too often, nonprofits approach the bank in the same way they have learned to approach a government contract or foundation officer—with a need, but with no carefully thought-through method for repayment.

Assuming you have otherwise met the "Five- C's" listed on the following page, why else might your loan be denied?

Weak Balance Sheet—If the liabilities side of your balance sheet exceeds your assets, you have what the bank will consider a "weak" balance sheet. Poor financial health is one of the most common reasons for loan denial.

Poor Credit Report—If your loan is denied because of a credit report, the bank is required by law to advise you of the credit bureau from which the report was obtained. Request copies of the report from the credit bureau and check it carefully for inaccuracies. If you find an error, write immediately to correct it. The Fair Credit Reporting Act gives you the right to insert a statement of up to 100 words in your report to explain credit problems. Be sure to keep copies for your files.

Insufficient Collateral—Even with good credit references and positive net assets, your loan may still be denied due to insufficient collateral. Although in limited circumstances a bank may choose to make an

---

The Five C's of Nonprofit Credit Analysis

Capacity   Where will the money come from to repay the loan?

Capital   What kind of "back-up" assets do you have if your primary source of payment fails?

Collateral   What assets will you pledge to secure the loan?

Conditions   What is the purpose of the loan? What is the current and projected financial climate for an organization like yours?

Character   How much confidence does the bank have in you as the responsible party for repaying the loan?

▼

unsecured loan, more often then not the bank will require security equal to or greater than the value of the loan. Nonprofits with government contracts, non-renewable foundation grants, and limited fixed assets frequently cannot produce sufficient collateral to pledge as security on a bank loan.

Although nonprofit managers have become much more financially astute over the last several years, the financial challenges they face have never been greater. Nonprofits eager to continue quality programs and services must seek new financial options to enhance traditional funding. Borrowing money is one such option.

Borrowing, however, is not for everyone. Like any source of income, loans come with strings attached—they must be repaid, with interest. Still, even with the carrying costs, many nonprofits find loans to be a reliable, economical source of working capital as they strive to achieve financial stability.

▼

FINANCIAL TROUBLE SHOOTING

More than ever before, nonprofit managers realize that their organization's mission, no matter how important, can't exist without solid financial support and management. As much as we'd like to hope otherwise, however, even the smartest nonprofit managers sometimes face circumstances that threaten their financial equilibrium.

Later in this chapter we'll look at early warning signs of financial trouble. First, though, let's do a quick check-up on your current financial health.

Taking Your Financial Pulse

A doctor considers a whole set of factors to determine your physical well-being. You can also examine several indicators to gauge your organization's financial health. The good news is that you can be financially healthy regardless of budget size. In fact, you could have a $50,000 budget and be in tip-top shape, while a multi-million dollar organization could be on the brink of financial disaster. Financial health is not about how much you have, but what you do with what you have. And the less you have, the more you need to make of it.

The following "financial health indicators" are based on The Stevens Group's 1990 study *The Financial Health of Minnesota's Nonprofits*, published by the Minnesota Nonprofits Assistance Fund. How well do you measure up?

Financially healthy nonprofits have sufficient financial resources to ensure stable programming. The two adjectives in this sentence—sufficient and stable—are the key words here. Nonprofits, like any business, need adequate income to meet program demands. Just as important, healthy nonprofits understand the value of continuity of service. A vibrant organization needs a stable source of income to continue its programming and ensure its credibility with clients, board members, and outside funders.

Financially healthy nonprofits have a ready source of internal cash—or access to cash—in times of shortfalls. Like any business, nonprofits must have cash to survive. Without cash, payrolls can't be met, taxes can't be paid, and services must be put on hold. Some organizations have their own savings surplus or reserve to handle inevitable income fluctuations. Other groups use borrowed money as a temporary solution. Either way, quick access to cash spells the difference between stable, uninterrupted services and crisis conditions.

Financially healthy nonprofits are committed to income-based, rather than budget-based, spending. Most nonprofits aspire to and value a balanced budget. Yet, some have not learned the relationship between having a balanced budget and adjusting the organization's actual expenses to match the income it has received. The spending patterns of financially healthy nonprofits are *income-based*. Financially healthy organizations do not overspend available income—whether it is budgeted or not.

Financially healthy nonprofits retain a positive cash fund balance at the end of the year. In the private sector, surplus (or "profit," as the sector usually refers to it) measures business success. A nonprofit's success is not as easily measured. Still, even though surplus does not indicate a nonprofit's *success*, it is a strong indicator of organizational health and stability.

Financially healthy nonprofits accumulate annual surpluses to use as a safety net in years when an unforeseen deficit does occur. Financially healthy organizations hold themselves accountable for developing strategies to handle deficits in years when financial resources are not as great as originally anticipated. They wisely find ways to make up for a current year's deficit by spending less in the following year(s) or by supplementing the shortfall with accumulated surpluses.

Financially healthy nonprofits have established—or plan to establish—an operating reserve to finance cash shortfalls and program growth. Operating reserves are a planned strategy for financial performance. They *anticipate* financial shortcomings and are generally established with board participation to meet those shortcomings. Reserves can be developed through an internally-funded savings plan or by funding depreciation. They can also be fundraised.

Seven Characteristics of Financially Healthy Nonprofits

1. Financially healthy nonprofits have sufficient financial resources to ensure stable programming.

2. Financially healthy organizations have a ready source of internal cash—or access to cash—in times of shortfalls.

3. Financially healthy organizations are committed to income-based, rather than budget-based, spending.

4. Financially healthy organizations retain a positive cash fund balance at the end of the year.

5. Financially healthy nonprofits accumulate annual surpluses to use as a safety net in years when an unforeseen deficit does occur.

6. Financially healthy organizations have established—or plan to establish—an operating reserve to finance cash shortfalls and program growth.

7. Financial healthy nonprofits have a board of directors and management that hold themselves responsible for the financial stability of the organization.

The Financial Health of Minnesota's Nonprofits, Minnesota Nonprofits Assistance Fund
Authored by Susan Kenny Stevens and Richard Hamer, The Stevens Group, Inc.
Copyright © 1990 All Rights Reserved.

Financially healthy nonprofits have a board of directors and management that hold themselves responsible for the financial stability of the organization. Although the prevailing opinion is that the board of directors alone is ultimately responsible for the success or failure of a nonprofit organization, in practice, it is often the executive director who *feels* and *takes* the responsibility. While some boards and managers may need training to increase their financial skills, lack of skill does not take the place of responsibility. The important issue is that *someone* takes responsibility for the success or failure of the nonprofit they are there to govern or manage.

As you can see, financial health is far more than "surviving" on a day-to-day basis. Financially healthy nonprofits meet the unexpected—whether good or bad—on their feet instead of on their knees. Unfortunately, many nonprofits think that "surviving" is enough. What they don't realize is that they could be financially hemorrhaging and not know it until it's too late. Like the *Titanic*, the ship may be sinking while everyone continues with life as usual.

Signs of Financial Trouble

Early detection is the name of the game here. Usually, the earliest sign of trouble is when a nonprofit does not have the cash to meet a scheduled payroll. But there are other early warning signs, too. Some are more obvious than others.

If you answer yes to one or more of the statements on the following page, *now* is the time to make a midcourse correction. Each of these warning signs has varying levels of severity. But each also has a remedy—if you deal with the problem in time. (Remember, getting into financial trouble is always easier than getting out!)

There are no easy answers to these problems. But the quicker you act and the more decisive the action, the greater the likelihood of warding off total disaster, or in the case of an existing loan, warding off default.

Early Warning Signs of Financial Trouble

1. Your organization consistently spends more money than it receives in revenue.

2. You're not paying payroll taxes in a timely fashion.

3. Payables—the amount you owe others—are mounting up and going unpaid.

4. You regularly dip into restricted or deferred funds for today's expenses, coming up short later when the special project is ready to go.

5. More than 50 percent of your accounts receivable—the money others owe you—are 120 days or older.

6. You consistently need to get an advance from the United Way or other contract source to meet today's expenses.

7. You have no idea how your organization got into such a financial mess, and you don't know how to begin to pull out of it.

8. You don't know how much the organization owes, and you don't know how to find out.

9. Lack of money has become the focus and dominant point of conversation at staff and board meetings.

10. You feel hopeless or are losing sleep at night because of the financial condition of your organization.

Cashing In: A Nonprofit's Introduction to Borrowing Money, Minnesota Nonprofits Assistance Fund
Authored by Susan Kenny Stevens, The Stevens Group, Inc.
Copyright © 1990 All Rights Reserved.

The first step to turning around a financially distressed organization is to admit there is a problem. Sometimes the expertise needed to help solve the overriding problem and its symptoms exists within the organization. Board and advisory committee members can often be very helpful in this process. At other times, however, outside technical assistance is needed.

Technical assistance is nothing more than practical, hands-on problem solving. Your banker or lender can be an excellent source for initial advice, especially because he or she has a vested interest in your organization's success. Other resources at your disposal include your auditor and outside financial consultants.

Choosing the Right Audit Firm

One financial resource that many nonprofits often overlook is their Certified Public Accountant (CPA). In addition to conducting your annual audit, a CPA can also provide valuable "trouble-shooting" advice for your organization.

The first step to getting your money's worth from your auditor is to make sure you hire the right one. Most nonprofits will have at least a couple of CPAs in their area from whom to choose. Here are four steps to help you find the right firm or individual for the job.

Narrow the Field. Develop a list of several reputable CPA firms that have experience providing financial services to other nonprofit organizations. To narrow the list, find firms that have experience with organizations in your specific field (arts, human service, economic development, etc.). Once you've narrowed down your list of choices, ask the remaining contenders to submit proposals for the services requested.

Interview Potential Firms. After you've received proposals, set up interviews with the firms you believe will provide your organization with the desired results. In the interview process, ask about the firm's experience with nonprofits similar in mission and size to your own organization. Find out about the individual who will oversee and perform the audit. What is that person's experience in nonprofit accounting? What is the likelihood of that person continuing to do the audit in subsequent years? Is the person willing and available to assist with questions or problems that may come up during the rest of the year when the audit is not in progress?

Evaluate Costs. The cost of an audit is always a major consideration. Keep in mind that you often get what you pay for—don't automatically choose the lowest bid. A "pro bono" audit is free, but it may raise red flags with funders if the accountant performing the audit doesn't understand nonprofit accounting or issues specific to your industry.

Put the Agreement in Writing. Once you've chosen a firm or an individual, ask for an engagement letter that details the following: (1) the work they are agreeing to perform; (2) the price of their services; and (3) any other items agreed upon, such as work you may need to complete before the audit can begin. You will need to sign this engagement letter before any work on the audit can commence.

Your auditor or CPA will typically be well-qualified to find a problem in your financial system and make recommendations on how to resolve it. Many times, however, a "system" problem is actually the symptom of a much larger issue. In this case, you would do well to hire a consultant to address the bigger picture of what is happening in your organization.

Even the smartest of nonprofit managers will sometimes find themselves in circumstances that threaten their financial equilibrium. Savvy money managers look for ways to anticipate and plan for such situations and keep an alert-eye to detect early warning signs of trouble. Smart money managers don't stop there, however. They are also willing to get outside help when needed, recognizing that other financial professionals— bankers, consultants, auditors—are a valuable resource to be utilized for the nonprofit's benefit.

▼

BECOMING TOMORROW'S NONPROFIT

S mart money management is a means to an end, not an end in itself. For nonprofits that effectively manage their precious resources, it simply means that they are positioning themselves to become the movers and shakers of the future, or what we like to call "tomorrow's nonprofits."

Tomorrow's nonprofits are smart—smart about who they are, where they're going, and the resources they need to get there. Being a smart money manager won't make much of a difference if your organization has no reason to exist. Equally true, having a mission won't make much of a difference if you don't know how to manage the resources you have.

In our experience, tomorrow's nonprofits share five common characteristics:

Tomorrow's Nonprofits Focus on Community. As society's original entrepreneurs, nonprofits have long filled gaps in community service left by both their private and public sector partners. To be well positioned for the future, nonprofits need to keep a vigilant outward-focus to ensure that community needs, rather than internal desires, drive programs and subsequent management and financial decisions. Fidelity to mission is easily defended, yet even the best missions calcify when pursued without attention to the marketplace. Results-oriented nonprofits will make client-focused, rather than self-focused, decisions.

Tomorrow's Nonprofits Invent the Future Before It Invents Them. The best way to predict the future is to invent it yourself. For nonprofits, this means taking control of your destiny rather than becoming a victim of circumstance. The first step toward inventing the future is to anticipate changes in the external environment and take stock of internal vulnerabilities. This requires an openness to the possibility that past programs and practices may not be suitable to your organization's future

Nonprofit Organizations

In the 1980s

"How To" ─────────────→ "Who For"

Activity ─────────────→ Results

Strategy ─────────────→ Purpose

Professionalize ─────────────→ Flexibility

Solidify Operations in Community ─────────────→ Make a Difference

Cash Reserves/Endowments ─────────────→ Working Capital

Own Programs ─────────────→ Strategic Alliances

In the 1990s

incarnation. Collaborations, partnerships, and shared administrative services are but the beginning of future reinventions for the results-oriented nonprofit.

Tomorrow's Nonprofits Stay Flexible and Ready for Change. Flexibility will undoubtedly emerge as the virtue of the 1990s. As one nonprofit manager put it, "I can sum up my 20 years in the nonprofit sector in five words: the finish line keeps changing." Nonprofits positioned for the future will be flexible, take change in stride, and build organizational cultures that are ready for change. Most importantly, results-oriented nonprofits will view change as the constant and their programs and activities as the variable in planning for the future accomplishment of their mission.

Tomorrow's Nonprofits Develop Results-Oriented Budgets. Nonprofits are not exempt from the current criticism pervading both government and philanthropic funders: "Who is better off because of our efforts?" Consequently, results-oriented budgeting—the relationship between dollars in and results out—needs to be added to existing program- and income-based budgeting techniques. As more and more foundation and government funders adopt outcome expectations, nonprofits will need a new method to show the positive relationship between a funder's investment and the ultimate benefit of those dollars on the community.

Tomorrow's Nonprofits Set Energetic but Realistic Goals. Entrepreneurial spirit has always been alive and well in the nonprofit sector. That spirit, coupled with the plethora of management techniques that have emerged over the last decade, provide nonprofits with the opportunity to "move and shake" their communities in an equally energetic but more informed manner. For some this will mean staking out new territory. For others, it means simply adopting new methods. But for all, a spirit of realism about the available level of reliable, sustainable financial support will be necessary to avoid the unforeseen pitfalls of the past.

It is our hope—no matter what your sector, clientele, budget size, or financial condition—that you are committed to becoming a nonprofit of tomorrow. Armed with a sense of possibility and realism, may you make the most of every opportunity and resource that you have.

Five Strategies For Tomorrow's Nonprofit

---

1. Refocus on Community

2. Invent the Future Before It Invents You

3. Stay Flexible and Ready for Change

4. Develop Results-Oriented Budgets

5. Set Energetic But Realistic Goals

Refocusing on Community: The 1994 Study on the Financial Health of Minnesota's Nonprofits
Published by The Stevens Group, Inc.

ACRONYMS

ARM	Adjustable rate mortgage
APR	Annual percentage rate
ATM	Automated teller machine
CD	Certificate of deposit
CPA	Certified public accountant
CRA	Community Reinvestment Act
EFT	Electronic funds transfer
FASB	Financial Accounting Standards Board
FDIC	Federal Deposit Insurance Corporation
GAAP	Generally Accepted Accounting Principles
NCUA	National Credit Union Administration
NOW	Negotiated order of withdrawal
PIN	Personal identification number
PRI	Program related investment
SAIF	Savings Association Insurance Fund
S&L	Savings and Loan Association

▼

GLOSSARY

Accessions—Additions, both purchased and donated, to collections held by museums, art galleries, botanical gardens, libraries and similar entities.

Account—A record of an organization's financial transactions maintained in a special book or ledger. Separate accounts are kept for assets, liabilities, net assets, revenues and expenses.

Account Number—An assigned number which provides numerical control over accounts and provides a convenient means of referring to the account.

Accounting Period—The period of time for which an operating statement is customarily prepared. Examples: a month (the most common accounting period), four weeks, a quarter (of a year), 26 weeks, a year, 52 weeks.

Accounting System—A network of procedures through which financial transactions and information are accumulated, classified in the accounts, recorded in the various books of account and reported in the financial statements.

Accounts Payable—A liability representing the amount owed to others for merchandise or services provided to the organization.

Accounts Receivable—An asset representing the amounts owed to the organization.

Accrual-Basis Accounting—An accounting system that recognizes expenses when they are incurred and revenues when they are earned, rather than when cash changes hands. It records amounts payable and amounts receivable in addition to recording transactions resulting from the exchange of cash.

Compiled by The Stevens Group with acknowledgment to the Public Management Institute and the Financial Accounting Standards Board.

Adjusting (Journal) Entry—The record made of an accounting transaction giving effect to the correction of an error, an accrual, a write-off, a provision for bad debts or depreciation, or the like.

Administrative Budget—A financial plan under which an organization carries on its day-to-day affairs under the common forms of administrative management; a budget. The term is usually employed in contradistinction to capital budget or program budget, where the plan covers transactions of a non-operating character.

Agency Fund—*See Custodian Funds.*

Allocate—To charge an item or group of items of revenue or cost to one or more objects, activities, processes, operations or products, in accordance with cost responsibilities, benefits received, or other readily identifiable measure of application or consumption.

Annual Percentage Rate (APR)—The finance charge on a loan over a one-year period, expressed as a percentage.

Asset—A resource, object, or right of measurable financial value (e.g., cash, securities, accounts receivable, land, building and equipment).

Audit—A series of procedures followed by a professional accountant used to test, on a selective basis, transactions and internal controls in effect, all with a view to forming an opinion on the fairness of the organization's annual financial statements.

Available Balance—The portion of a customer's account balance on which the bank has placed no restrictions, making it available for immediate withdrawal.

Average Daily Balance—The average amount of money that a customer keeps on deposit, determined by adding the daily balances of the account for a given length of time and dividing the total by the number of days covered.

Balance Sheet—The financial statement that presents an organization's financial position at a certain specified date. It lists assets, liabilities and net assets. May also be referred to as the *Statement of Position.*

Balanced Budget—A budget in which forward expenditures for a given period are matched by expected revenues for the same period.

Bank—*See Commercial Bank.*

Board-Designated Net Assets—A designation that is self-imposed by the board on a certain segment of its unrestricted net assets for some specific activity or project that is to be carried out in the future. Board designation has no legal significance.

Bond—A long-term debt instrument. The issuer (a corporation, unit of government, or other legal entity) promises to repay the stated principal at a specified date and agrees to pay a specific rate of interest.

Bridge Loan—A short-term loan made in anticipation of longer term financing.

Budget—A financial plan which estimates the monetary receipts and expenditures for an operating period. Budgets may be directed toward project or program activities and are primarily used as a comparison and control feature against the actual financial results.

Capital Additions—Gifts, grants, bequests, investment income and gains on investments, restricted either permanently or for a period of time by parties outside of the organization to endowment and loan funds. Such additions also include similar resources restricted for fixed asset additions but only to the extent expended during the year.

Capitalizing an Asset—The process of recording the cost of land, buildings, and equipment as fixed assets, rather than expensing them when they were initially acquired.

Cash-Basis Accounting—An accounting system that records only those events that involve the exchange of cash and ignores transactions that do not involve cash.

Cash-Disbursements Journal—The journal recording all financial transactions involving the disbursement of cash.

Cash Flow—The difference between cash receipts and disbursements over a given period of time.

Cash Flow Loan—A short-term loan made to bridge the gap between an immediate need for cash and a pending, verified receivable.

Cash Flow Statement—A statement of cash income and outgo between two given dates.

Cash Receipts Journal—The journal recording financial transactions involving the receipt of cash.

Certificate of Deposit (CD)—A formal receipt issued by a bank for a specified amount of money, left with the bank for a certain amount of time. CDs usually bear interest, payable at maturity or after a specified minimum notice of intent to withdraw.

Certified Public Accountant (CPA)—An accountant licensed by the state to certify financial statements.

Chart of Accounts—A list that organizes the agency's accounts in a systematic manner, usually by account number, to facilitates the preparation of financial statements and periodic financial reports.

Collateral—An asset which is pledged to a lender until the loan is repaid. In case of default, the lender legally owns the right to obtain or sell the collateral as payment on the loan.

Collections—Works of art, botanical and animal specimens, books and other items held for display or study by museums and similar institutions.

Commercial Bank—By law, an institution that accepts demand deposits and makes commercial loans.

Community Reinvestment Act (CRA)—A law passed in 1977 that requires banks to meet the credit needs of their communities, including the low- and moderate-income sections of those communities.

Comparative Statements—Balance sheets, income or flow statements, or other accounting summaries juxtaposed for the purpose of contrasting the financial characteristics of an organization from one period to another.

Conditional Promise to Give—A written or oral agreement to contribute cash or other assets to another entity in which the contribution depends on the occurrence of a specified future or uncertain event to bind the promisor.

Contributed Services—Contributed services are recognized as revenue only if they create or add value to a non-financial asset such as capital improvements to a building or office space; or if they require specialized skills that would typically need to be purchased if not provided by donation. Organizations recognizing contributed services are required to disclose a description of the service received by the program or activity, nature and extent of the services, and the amount recognized as revenues.

Contribution—A transfer of cash or other assets to another entity in which the transfer is unconditional, made or received voluntarily, and is nonreciprocal.

Cost Center—An organizational division, department, or unit having common supervision.

CPA—*See Certified Public Accountant.*

CRA—*See Community Reinvestment Act.*

Credit Union—A voluntary cooperative association of individuals having some common bond, organized to accept deposits, extend loans, and provide other financial services.

Creditor—One who is due money from another.

Custodian Funds—Funds received and held by an organization as fiscal agent for others. *Syn: Agency Fund.*

Debit and Credit—Technical book-keeping terms referring to the two sides of a financial occurrence. The increase or decrease effect on the account depends on the type of account. The debits must equal the credits for any given financial occurrence.

Debt—Borrowed funds from individuals, banks or other institutions, generally secured with a note, which in turn may be secured by a lien against property or other assets. Ordinarily, the note states repayment and interest provisions.

Deferred Revenue—Revenue received before it is earned. (For example, advance ticket sales or membership dues.)

Deficit—1. Expenses and losses in excess of related income; an operating loss. 2. An accumulation of operating losses ("negative" retained income).

Demand Deposit—Funds that may be withdrawn from a bank without advance notice. Checking accounts are the most common form of demand deposits.

Depreciating an Asset—The process by which the cost of a fixed asset is expensed over its useful life. The annual charge to expense is referred to as depreciation expense.

Designated Net Assets—Unrestricted net assets set aside by action of the governing board for specific purposes. *See also Quasi-Endowment Funds, Board-Designated Net Assets.*

Double-Entry Bookkeeping—A method of bookkeeping that recognizes a two-way, self-balancing, debit/credit entry for all financial occurrences.

Earned Income—The amount received for goods or services delivered and for which no future liability is anticipated.

Encumbrances—Commitments in the form of orders, contracts, and similar items that will become payable when goods are delivered or services rendered.

Endowment—A type of donor restriction on contributed assets that stipulates that the assets endowed must remain intact either temporarily (until a stated period of time has passed or a specific occurrence has taken place) or permanently. The revenue earned from such assets is unrestricted unless specified otherwise by the donor or state law.

Exchange Transaction—A reciprocal transfer of assets in which the resource provider receives equal or commensurate value in exchange for the transferred assets.

Expendable Fund—A fund that is available to finance an organization's program and supporting services, including both unrestricted and restricted amounts.

Expenditure—The incurring of a liability, the payment of cash, or the transfer of property for the purpose of acquiring an asset or service or settling a loss.

Expense—Asset expended resulting in a decrease in net assets.

FASB—The Financial Accounting Standards Board (FASB) is the governing board that formulates authoritative accounting standards for nongovernmental agencies. These standards, which encompass accounting rules, procedures, and applications, define accepted accounting practice and are referred to as *Generally Accepted Accounting Principles (GAAP)*.

Federal Deposit Insurance Corporation (FDIC)—The agency of the federal government, established in 1933, to provide insurance protection for depositors at FDIC member institutions.

Fiduciary Relationship—A relationship between persons based on trust and confidence. A fiduciary, such as a trustee, owes a duty of upmost good faith.

Fixed Asset—An asset that has a relatively long useful life, usually several years or more, such as land, building and equipment.

Float—The dollar amount of deposited cash items that have been given immediate, provisional credit but are in the process of collection from drawee banks. Also known as uncollected funds.

Functional Classification—A classification of expenses that accumulates expenses according to the purpose for which costs are incurred. The primary functional classifications are program and supporting services.

Fund—An accounting entity established for the purpose of accounting for resources used for specific activities or objectives in accordance with special purposes as restricted by a donor or as designated by the organization. Each organization can choose to account by funds based on its own needs to track specific financial activity.

Fund Accounting—An accounting system that divides the accounts into separate groupings that reflect various organizational or donor-restricted purposes and that indicate how assets were utilized for these specified purposes.

Fund Group—A group of funds of similar character, for example operating funds, endowment funds and annuity and life income funds.

Funds Held in Trust by Others—Resources held and administered at the direction of the donor by an outside trustee for the benefit of the organization.

Generally Accepted Accounting Principles (GAAP)—Accounting standards for non-governmental agencies which encompass accounting rules, procedures and applications, and define accepted accounting practice. *See also FASB.*

Grants—An unconditional promise to give assets to an organization by an individual or another organization. Grants must be recognized in the year the unconditional promise to give is received. *See also Multi-Year Grants.*

Guarantee—To make oneself liable for the debt of another.

Guarantor—One who promises to make good if another fails to pay or otherwise perform an assigned or contractual task.

Income—Assets received resulting in an increase in net assets.

Income Statement—*See Statement of Income and Expenses.*

Increase (Decrease) in Net Assets—The difference between "Total Revenue" and "Total Expenses" representing net financial results of operations for the period.

Interest—Money paid for the use of money.

Interest Accrued—Interest which has been earned, but is not due or payable.

Interest Write-Down—A subsidy or reduction in the market rate of interest.

Interfund Receivable (Payable)—An amount that is due from one fund to another.

Interfund Transaction/Transfer—A transfer of assets from one fund to another.

Internal Controls—The plan of organization, procedures and records designed to enhance the safeguarding of assets and the reliability of records of an organization.

Inventory—An asset consisting of goods purchased and/or produced and held for resale.

Investment Pool—Assets of several funds pooled or consolidated for investment purposes.

Investment Revenue—The revenue derived from the investment of assets. It includes interest, dividends, and realized and unrealized capital gains (net of losses).

Liability—A claim on the assets by an outsider representing a financial obligation. Liabilities include accounts payable, accrued expenses and loans.

Line of Credit—Either secured or unsecured, an agreement which ordinarily is renewed on an annual basis where a bank holds funds available for the use of a business. Usually an unsecured line will have to be completely paid out once a year.

Liquid Assets—Cash in banks and on hand, and other cash assets not set aside for specific purposes other than the payment of a current liability, or a readily marketable investment.

Liquidity—The quality that makes an asset quickly and easily convertible into cash.

Load—The portion of the offering price of shares of open-end investment companies which covers sales commissions and all other costs of distribution.

Loan—The lending of a sum of money by a lender to a borrower, to be repaid with a certain amount of interest. May be either secured or unsecured, on a time, demand, or installment basis. *Secured loans* are backed by collateral which the bank may claim in case of default by the maker; *time loans* have a fixed or determinable maturity; demand loans are terminable at the option of either the lender or the borrower; *installment loans* are repaid in regular installments at fixed intervals.

Loan Application—A form used to record the formal request for a loan by a borrower.

Market Value—The realizable amount for which an asset can be sold in the open market.

Minimum Balance—The amount that a depositor must have on deposit in an account to qualify for special services or escape service charges.

Modified Cash-Basis Accounting—The same as cash-basis accounting except for certain items which are treated on an accrual basis (e.g., depreciation and payroll taxes). This is also known as a "hybrid method."

Mortgage Loan—A loan with property pledged as collateral.

Multi-Year Grant—An unconditional promise to give grant assets to an organization by an individual or another organization that extends beyond one year. These grants must be recognized in the year the unconditional promise to give is received and must be recorded using a discount rate to measure the present value of the estimated future cash flow.

Net Assets—The difference between total assets (what is owned) and total liabilities (what is owed).

Net Investment in Plant—The total carrying value of all property, plant and equipment, and related liabilities, exclusive of real properties held for investment.

Nonexpendable Additions—*See Capital Additions.*

Object Classification of Expenses—A method of classifying expenditures according to their natural classification such as salaries and wages, employee benefits, supplies, purchased services and so forth.

Obligation—The legal responsibility and duty of the debtor (the obligor) to pay a debt when due, and the legal right of the creditor (the obligee) to enforce payment in the event of default.

Operating Reserve—An unrestricted net asset used to stabilize an organization's finances.

Permanently Restricted Net Asset—A donor-imposed restriction that stipulates contributed assets be maintained permanently. Unless otherwise stipulated by the donor or state law, the organization is permitted to use up or expend part or all of the income derived from permanently restricted assets.

Pledge—A receivable representing a specified sum that an individual or organization has promised to contribute.

Principal—A sum lent or employed as a fund or investment, as distinguished from its income or profits. In lending, the original amount of the total due and payable at a certain date.

Program Services—The programs and activities carried out which represent the principle reason for the organization's existence.

Promise to Give—A written or oral agreement to contribute cash or other assets to another entity. A promise to give must contain sufficient verifiable documentation that a promise was made and received.

Property, Plant & Equipment Fund—A fund group that may contain all fixed assets as well as the assets that are donor restricted or board designated for the purpose of purchasing fixed assets.

Prospectus—The official circular which describes the shares of an investment company and offers them for sale. Also used to refer to a selling document used for nonprofit fundraising that provides a summary description of an organization's goals, needs, history, financial information and personnel.

Quasi-Endowment Funds—Unrestricted funds which the governing board of an organization, rather than a donor, has determined are to be retained and invested. The governing board has the right to decide at any time to expend the principal of such funds. *See Designated Net Assets, Board-Designated Net Assets.*

Refinance—To replace one loan with another, usually in order to extend the maturity, or to consolidate several notes.

Refundable Advance—An asset which is transferred to an organization before a condition has been substantially met. Refundable advances are recorded as a liability on the balance sheet until conditions are met, at which time they are recognized as revenue.

Restricted Asset—An asset that has legal restrictions imposed on its use by outsiders.

Revenue—Assets earned or income from services performed or goods sold.

Revolving Line of Credit—Similar to a line of credit, except it need not be paid out annually.

Savings and Loan Association (S&L)—A federally or state-chartered thrift institution that accepts various types of deposits and uses them primarily for home mortgage loans.

Second Mortgage—A mortgage which is made on property which already had a mortgage placed upon it. The first mortgage has priority or claim over the second mortgage.

Secured—Guaranteed as to payment by the pledge of something valuable.

Short-Term Debt—Interest-bearing debt payable within one year from the date of issue.

Statement of Activities—*See Statement of Income and Expenses.*

Statement of Cash Flows—The financial statement which provides relevant information about the cash receipts and cash payments of an organization during a period.

Statement of Functional Expenses—The financial statement that details the specific types of expenses by object (i.e., rent, salaries, etc.) that were incurred in each of the programs and supporting activities delineated on the Statement of Activities.

Statement of Income and Expenses—The financial statement that summarizes the financial activity of an organization for a given period of time. It presents the income, expenses and changes in net assets for the period.

Statement of Position—*See Balance Sheet.*

Stock—A certificate evidencing ownership in a corporate enterprise.

Support—Income from voluntary contributions and grants.

Support Services—Auxiliary activities that provide the various support functions essential to achieve program services.

Take Out Loan—Permanent loan on real property which replaces an interim loan.

Temporarily Restricted Net Asset—A donor-imposed restriction on contributed assets which will eventually either expire with the passage of time or will be fulfilled through action by the organization.

Unconditional Promise to Give—A "no strings attached" written or oral agreement to contribute cash or other assets to another entity.

Unrealized Gain (or Loss)—The amount by which the market value of an asset exceeds (or is less than) the original cost of that asset.

Unrestricted Net Assets—Sometimes called operating funds or general funds, this net asset group contains the assets on which there are no donor restrictions and from which the bulk of financial activity is usually handled.

Unsecured Loan—A loan made without collateral, but rather on the signature of the borrower.

Write-offs—An instrument which has been determined to be uncollectible, since there are no known visible assets available with which to liquidate the obligation.

Working Capital—That portion of an organization's assets which is not invested in fixed assets, but is kept liquid to care for day to day working needs.

INDEX

▼